A Friendly Guide to MATTHEW'S GOSPEL

Dorothy A Lee

garratt
PUBLISHING

Published in Australia by
Garratt Publishing
32 Glenvale Crescent
Mulgrave, Vic. 3170

www.garrattpublishing.com.au

Copyright © Dorothy Lee 2013

All rights reserved. Except as provided by the Australian copyright law, no part of this book may be reproduced in any way without permission in writing from the publisher.

Design and typesetting by Lynne Muir
Text editing by Geraldine Corridon
Images: Thinkstock.com
p. 4. Caravaggio (Merisi, Michelangelo da (1571-1610): *Calling of Saint Matthew*, 1598-1601. Rome, Church of San Luigi dei Francesi. Oil on canvas. cm 322 x 340.- © 2012. Photo Scala, Florence

Scripture quotations are drawn from the *New Revised Standard Version of the Bible,* copyright © 1989 by the Division of Christian Education of the National Council of the Churches of Christ in the USA. Used by permission. All rights reserved.

Nihil Obstat: Reverend Gerard Diamond MA (Oxon), LSS, D.Theol, Diocesan Censor

Imprimatur: Monsignor Greg Bennet, Vicar General

Date: 4 August 2012

The Nihil Obstat and Imprimatur are official declarations that a book or pamphlet is free of doctrinal or moral error. No implication is contained therein that those who have granted the Nihil Obstat and Imprimatur agree with the contents, opinions or statements expressed. They do not necessarily signify that the work is approved as a basic text for catechetical instruction.

9781921946332

Cataloguing in Publication information for this title is available from the National Library of Australia. www.nla.gov.au

The author and publisher gratefully acknowledge the permission granted to reproduce the copyright material in this book. Every effort has been made to trace copyright holders and to obtain their permission for the use of copyright material. The publisher apologises for any errors or omissions in the above list and would be grateful if notified of any corrections that should be incorporated in future reprints or editions of this book.

Garratt Publishing has included on its website a page for special notices in relation to this and our other publications.

Please visit www.garrattpublishing.com.au

FOR MARGARET

CONTENTS

Preface..3

Who, When, Where?.........................5

Jesus and the Disciples......................7

Matthew's Way of Telling Jesus' Story...10

Jesus' Birth: Matthew 1:1–2:23..13

Jesus Prepares for his Ministry: Matthew 3:1–4:23............................16

Jesus' Ministry in Word and Deed: Matthew 5:1–16:12..........................19

Jesus' Journey to Jerusalem: Matthew 16:13–20:34.....................28

Jesus' Days in Jerusalem: Matthew 21:1–25:46.......................36

Jesus' Death and Resurrection: Matthew 26:1–28:20........................42

PREFACE

I would like to thank John Garratt for placing this challenge before me and for this wonderful project as a whole: an effort to educate the people of God in their faith. I have enjoyed writing it very much, and hope you enjoy reading it and find it accessible. I do hope, too, you'll feel free to disagree: to have the text of Matthew open in front of you, and to form your own opinions. You might also like to have a look at Mark and see how Matthew has edited Mark in so many, fascinating ways. The bible passages quoted in this book are from the *New Revised Standard Version Bible*.

I want to thank also my colleagues at Trinity College and within MCD University of Divinity for their support of me and of this project.

I also owe much to my extended family, both in Australia and in the UK. One of them, in particular, stands out for me over these past months: my cousin, Margaret Marks, in England. It is to her that I dedicate this *Friendly Guide*.

Dorothy A. Lee
Feast Day of St Alban, first British martyr, second century AD

MATTHEW IS THE LONGEST OF ALL THE FOUR GOSPELS, WITH 28 CHAPTERS AND JUST OVER 1000 VERSES.

WE DON'T KNOW WHO WROTE MATTHEW'S GOSPEL, THOUGH LATER TRADITION SAYS THAT THIS MATTHEW WAS THE TAX COLLECTOR WHO BECAME AN APOSTLE (9:9; 10:3).

Caravaggio (Merisi, Michelangelo da (1571-1610): *Calling of Saint Matthew*, 1598-1601. Rome, Church of San Luigi dei Francesi. Oil on canvas. cm 322 x 340.- © 2012. Photo Scala, Florence

WHO, WHEN, WHERE?

Matthew's Gospel is the first book of the New Testament. That's not because Matthew was written first. The Letters of Paul were most likely written before any of the Gospels, and Mark was probably written before any of the other Gospels, including Matthew.

The first three Gospels are close to each other and are generally called *Synoptic Gospels*, because they can be viewed side by side ('syn-' means 'together' and 'optic' means 'to see'). The Gospel of John is different in many ways: in the stories, events and even some of the characters. Although it overlaps with the Synoptic Gospels, it represents a different tradition about Jesus.

By viewing the Synoptic Gospels together, we can see the way in which Matthew has made use of Mark — where he has added stories or sayings, what he has left out and how he has reorganised the Markan material. This is very helpful for us. Sometimes we can see at a glance what Matthew is trying to emphasise.

It is likely that Matthew made use of a second source, called 'Q'. This document has never actually been discovered. It's a hypothesis — an intelligent guess — based on the fact that Matthew and Luke share in common a good deal of the sayings of Jesus which are not found in Mark. These shared sayings often occur in different contexts in Matthew and Luke, suggesting they have used a common source independent of each other. Matthew also has material of his own, from the traditions of his community, which he has added to create a unique account of Jesus.

We speak commonly of 'Matthew' doing this and that in his writing, but we don't really know who this Matthew was. Later tradition identifies him with the tax collector in Matt 9:9 (called 'Levi' in Mk 2:14), and with the apostles, named at Matt 10:3. However, nothing in the Gospel tells us that this is the Matthew who wrote the Gospel.

Furthermore, if Mark's Gospel was written between 65 and 75 AD, we would expect Matthew to be later: probably in the 80s. This makes it less likely that the author was an eyewitness of Jesus' ministry.

Where Matthew was written is equally unknown and nothing in the Gospel points to its location. Some think Antioch in Syria is a reasonable guess. Antioch was a Greek-speaking city, largely Gentile, but with a Jewish population. A Christian community was founded there (Acts 13:1). Other places in the New Testament suggest that this Christian group had a strongly Jewish identity, but included Gentiles (Acts 11:19–20; Gal 2:11–14).

This picture of a Jewish–Christian community, within a non-Jewish city, seems to fit Matthew's Gospel and its context. Antioch in Syria is probably as good a guess as any.

> MATTHEW IS THE ONLY GOSPEL TO MENTION EXPLICITLY THE 'CHURCH'. HE IS VERY MUCH THE THEOLOGIAN OF THE CHURCH, WHICH PROBABLY EXPLAINS WHY HIS GOSPEL IS FIRST IN THE NEW TESTAMENT.

> MATTHEW DEPENDS FOR HIS
> INFORMATION MAINLY ON
> THE GOSPEL OF MARK.
> MOST OF MARK'S CONTENT IS FOUND
> IN MATTHEW.

Jesus and the Disciples

In telling the story of Jesus, Matthew tells us the meaning of his life, death, and resurrection. What emerges from this portrait is a Jesus whose birth is divine, whose ministry is acclaimed by God and whose death and resurrection are the result of God's will. At the same time, Jesus is undeniably human. He has a mother, brothers and sisters; he has friends; and he struggles to obey the will of God.

Jesus also identifies with human suffering, with our temptations, with our distress. He shows compassion for those who suffer and are rejected. He allows himself to endure the same things. He lives our life and dies our death, forging for us and our humanity a new path, a new capacity to be who and what we were created to be.

> **Although Matthew is interpreting and editing the story of Jesus, the content itself goes back to Jesus himself and the things he said and did.**

Behind Jesus, in Matthew's Gospel, with his love of the Law of Moses and his desire to fulfil God's will, stands the figure of God. In Matthew, God is gracious and, above all, good. He shows mercy to all, regardless of how they respond, irrespective of who they are. He is a God of forgiveness, whose generosity is sometimes crazy and illogical by human standards.

At the same time, Matthew's God is demanding. He calls for the perfection of love, seen especially in love of our enemies. God summons people to obedience, to fulfil their part in the covenant. God also calls for authenticity of life: a consistency of word and deed, inner and outer, the heart and the life. God calls for poverty of spirit, generosity and the forgiveness of others. In other words, God calls for an authentic living out of the Law, the Law as interpreted and lived by Jesus himself.

Matthew is also concerned with discipleship. This is the only Gospel which explicitly uses the word 'church' (*ekklêsia*). Jesus calls the twelve apostles, and particularly Peter, as the founding members of the church — those leaders on whose testimony later generations will build. Yet the church is not a hierarchy in Matthew. The authority given to Peter (16:19) is later given to the whole community in shared leadership (18:18). The church is not just the gathered apostles, but also the coming together of 'two or three' (18:20), the ordinary people whose well-being is paramount with God.

The disciples are presented in a more kindly light than they are in Mark. While they fail, and fail often, Jesus is gentle in response to their failures. They are treated as those of 'little faith' rather than of no faith. They are a mix of good and bad, understanding and misunderstanding, courage and cowardice. They follow Jesus faithfully throughout the Gospel, striving —

> **Chapter and verse divisions are not part of the original text of Matthew's Gospel (or of any other book in the Bible). Chapters were introduced in the thirteenth century, and verses in the sixteenth century.**

> THE WORD 'KINGDOM' REFERS PRIMARILY TO GOD'S SOVEREIGN, RULING ACTIVITY: GOD AS KING. ONLY IN A SECONDARY SENSE DOES IT REFER TO A DOMAIN, A PLACE, FOR WHICH DISCIPLES WORK. OFTEN WE USE THE TRANSLATION 'REIGN' INSTEAD OF 'KINGDOM' TO EMPHASISE THIS POINT.

often enough against their own instincts — to understand him. In the end, however, they fail him. Judas betrays him, Peter denies him, and the others flee. None of the apostles are with Jesus in his final agony and death.

Of all characters in Matthew, Peter shows most clearly this strange combination. He is spontaneous and courageous enough to ask Jesus to call him from the boat onto the water. But, as soon as he does, he loses sight of Jesus and begins to sink in terror at the wind and the waves (14:28–30). At one moment, he is the 'rock of the church', commended for his insight into Jesus' identity (16:16–17). The next moment, he is trying to turn Jesus from the path of suffering, and Jesus names him 'Satan', because he is blocking the path to the kingdom (16:22–23).

Yet the disciples' failure, especially at the cross, is not the last word. At the Last Supper, knowing that they will fail him, Jesus gives them the gift of his body and blood, the sign of the covenant to be sealed in his blood (26:26–29). This covenant is for 'the forgiveness of sins' (26:28). Jesus understands that, with the Shepherd struck down, the sheep will scatter (26:31).

In the end, the apostles are restored and, in all their doubts, are commissioned by the risen Christ and sent out on mission (28:16–20). Despite their sinking in the stormy seas, the hand of Jesus stretches out to clasp them and restore them. They are renewed and empowered by his sustaining grasp.

16 Now the eleven disciples went to Galilee, to the mountain to which Jesus had directed them. 17 When they saw him, they worshiped him; but some doubted. 18 And Jesus came and said to them, "All authority in heaven and on earth has been given to me. 19 Go therefore and make disciples of all nations, baptizing them in the name of the Father and of the Son and of the Holy Spirit, 20 and teaching them to obey everything that I have commanded you. And remember, I am with you always, to the end of the age." (Matthew 28:16–20)

The Twelve are not the only disciples in this Gospel. There are also women disciples, first hinted at in Matthew's genealogy, with the unexpected presence of four women, and Mary of Nazareth (1:1–18). Women emerge positively from the Gospel of Matthew, even if they are few in number. Most conspicuous are the Galilean women who, we learn at the end of the Passion narrative, have followed Jesus from Galilee to Jerusalem.

These women do not desert or deny him, but remain faithful — near the cross and at the tomb, witnesses to Jesus' death, burial and resurrection. The two Marys, Mary Magdalene and 'the other Mary', come to the tomb on Easter morning and believe the message of the angel. As they run to proclaim the good news, they are met by Jesus himself and, without question, worship him. They faithfully carry out their commission.

In the end, the disciples do not entirely fail in this Gospel. Their success is the result partly of their faith, but more importantly the presence and power of Jesus, who calls them, forgives them, and strengthens them to be his witnesses and to proclaim the gospel to 'all nations'.

THE GOSPEL WAS WRITTEN PROBABLY ABOUT 50 YEARS AFTER JESUS' DEATH AND RESURRECTION, AND IT REFLECTS A LATER SITUATION IN THE LIFE OF THE EARLY CHURCH.

Matthew's Way of Telling the Story of Jesus

Matthew's main source, Mark, has a clear structure: the prologue (Mk 1:1–1:15), Jesus' ministry in and around Galilee (Mk 1:16–8:21), his change of direction and journey to Jerusalem (Mk 8:22–10:52), and the events in Jerusalem — conflict, arrest, trial, death and empty tomb (Mk 11:1–16:8). Despite following Mark, Matthew's structure is more complicated. This is partly because of the changes and additions he makes to Mark.

Some structural points are clear. Matthew has five great discourses that run like the pillars of a cathedral through the Gospel narrative. These begin with the Sermon on the Mount (5:1–7:29), followed by the Mission Discourse (10:1–42), the Parables (13:1–52), the Community Discourse (18:1–34), and the Apocalyptic Discourse (24:1–46). Each ends with a phrase such as 'when Jesus had finished … saying (all) these things/parables' or 'instructing his twelve disciples' (7:28a, 11:1a, 13:53a, 19:1a, 26:1a). This makes the divisions plain to see.

Furthermore, the parallel between the five discourses and the first five books of Moses — the Pentateuch or Torah — should not be missed. Matthew sees Jesus as standing in the tradition of Moses, the Law-giver. Structural features have theological meaning.

Matthew's Gospel is structured around five discourses or sermons, which contain the essence of Jesus' teaching. In between the discourses are the stories of Jesus' ministry.

At the same time, Matthew alternates these great slabs of teaching with stories from Jesus' ministry. This is particularly apparent in the healing stories, which follow the Sermon on the Mount (7:28–9:35), though it is also true of the rest of Matthew's Gospel.

In this sense, Matthew demonstrates that word and deed belong together in Jesus' ministry. Unlike the portrayal of the religious authorities, with their hypocrisy — teaching one thing while doing another —Jesus is truly authentic: he lives out what he teaches without hypocrisy. He teaches that 'justice and mercy and faith' belong at the heart of the Law (23:23), and this is how he lives his life. Once again, Matthew's structure reflects his theology.

Matthew also loves grouping things in three. The Sermon on the Mount, for example, is full of such groups: e.g. almsgiving, prayer, prayer (6:1–18). The miracles of the following chapters are also organised in threes: three groups of three miracle stories, with other material in between each group (8:1–17; 8:23–9:8; 9:18–34).

Another feature of Matthew is the place of mountains. Six times in the Gospel, Jesus ascends a mountain. He is taken to a high mountain by the devil in the Temptation (4:8). His first discourse occurs on a mountain (5:1, 8:1). He ascends a mountain to pray after the first feeding story (14:23) and before the second feeding story (15:29). He takes Peter, James, and John up a high mountain for the Transfiguration (17:1, 9). Finally he appears to the apostles on a mountain in Galilee after his resurrection (28:16).

Mountains in the ancient world are places associated with the divine. In the Old Testament, they are places of revelation. Moses, in particular, is associated with Mount Sinai and the giving of the Law: God's ultimate act of self-revelation in the exodus story (Exod 24, 34).

Yet, while Matthew draws parallels between Jesus and Moses, Jesus far exceeds Moses. He speaks and acts in this Gospel with a direct authority, he possesses an identity that surpasses Moses. The mountains in Matthew emphasise the similarities with Moses and the greater status of Jesus. Moses is a positive figure for Matthew, and Jesus upholds the Law in word and deed (5:17–18). At the same time, in Jesus, God's self-revelation is complete, fulfilled, final.

There are other structural elements in Matthew. The dynamic between Jew and Gentile is fascinating as it develops in this Gospel. Jesus' ministry is primarily to 'the lost sheep of the house of Israel' (10:6, 15:24). Yet that changes as Jesus' ministry progresses. The Gospel, which is strongly Jewish–Christian, is framed by references to Gentiles: the coming of the Magi in the birth stories (2:1–12), and the command of the Risen Jesus to make disciples of 'all nations' or 'all Gentiles' (28:19).

A further structural element — and here Matthew is following Mark — is that Jesus first reveals his Passion, death, and resurrection in the middle of the Gospel, followed by the Transfiguration (16:13–17:13). In typical fashion, Matthew gives these two central episodes his own colouring. But the centre for Matthew is the revelation of Jesus as both the suffering and also the glorious Beloved Son.

> THE SERMON ON THE MOUNT IS LARGELY PUT TOGETHER BY MATTHEW HIMSELF. LUKE HAS AN EQUIVALENT SERMON ON THE PLAIN, BUT IT IS MUCH SHORTER THAN MATTHEW'S AND NOT LOCATED ON A MOUNTAIN.

JESUS' MISSION IN MATTHEW IS FIRST OF ALL TO THE JEWISH PEOPLE, AND ONLY LATER OPENS UP TO INCLUDE THE GENTILES.

Because Matthew partly follows Mark, and partly goes his own way, the structure of the Gospel is more difficult to work out. The earliest manuscripts give no indication of structure for Matthew, or for any of the Gospels. They have no chapters and verses, and there are not even spaces between words! So that doesn't help. However, like a good storyteller, Matthew works in a purposeful way. He knows what he is doing and where he is going.

The following structure divides the Gospel into six sections, tracing through Jesus' ministry, in word and action, from his birth to his resurrection:

I. Coming of Jesus as Christ and Son of God (Matt 1:1–4:11)

- Infancy stories — 1:1–2:23
- Jesus' baptism — 3:1–17
- Jesus' temptation — 4:1–11

II. Jesus' Teaching and Healing Ministry (Matt 4:12–11:30)

- Program of Jesus' ministry — 4:12–17
- Call of first disciples — 4:18–25
- Jesus' teaching ministry: 1st Discourse — 5:1–7:27
- Jesus' healing ministry — 7:28–9:35
- Mission of the disciples: 2nd Discourse — 10:1–42
- Messianic question, judgment and invitation to discipleship — 11:1–30

III. Jesus Confronts his Opponents (Matt 12:1–16:12)

- Conflict with Pharisees — 12:1–45
- Jesus' family — 12:46–50
- Parables of kingdom: 3rd Discourse — 13:1–52
- Rejection of Jesus and death of John the Baptist — 13:53–14:12
- Community of disciples and response of Pharisees — 14:13–16:12

IV. Jesus Journeys to Jerusalem (Matt 16:13–20:34)

- Peter's declaration at Cæsarea Philippi — 16:13–20
- First Passion prediction cycle: — 16:21–17:20
    - Jesus as suffering Messiah (16:21–28)
    - Transfiguration (17:1–13)
    - Healing of demonised boy (17:14–20)
- Second Passion prediction cycle: — 17:22–20:16
    - Jesus as suffering Messiah (17:22–23)
    - Payment of temple tax (17:24–27)
    - Life of new community: 4th Discourse (18:1–34)
    - Teaching on divorce, children, wealth and work (19:1–20:16)
- Third Passion prediction cycle: — 20:17–34
    - Jesus as suffering Messiah (20:17–19)
    - Request of mother of James and John (20:20–28)
    - Healing of two blind men (20:29–34)

V. Jesus' Days in Jerusalem (Matt 21:1–25:46)

- Triumphal entry — 21:1–11
- Conflict with authorities — 21:12–22:46
- Denouncing of scribes and Pharisees — 23:1–39
- Apocalyptic discourse: 5th Discourse — 24:1–25:46

VI. Jesus' Death and Resurrection (Matt 26:1–28:20)

- Jesus' arrest, trial and death — 26:1–27:66
- Jesus' resurrection — 28:1–15
- Commissioning of disciples — 28:16–20

Jesus' Birth: Matthew 1:1–2:23

Matthew tells the story of Jesus' birth in his own way, rather different from that of Luke (Matt 1–2, Lk 1–2). The other Gospels, Mark and John, have no birth stories. Matthew and Luke have a good deal in common, despite the differences. They tell of Mary's pregnancy before her marriage to Joseph, the child's miraculous conception, God's voice speaking through angels, Jesus' birth in Bethlehem, the reign of King Herod the Great and Jesus' upbringing in Nazareth.

> LUKE AND MATTHEW TELL DIFFERENT STORIES OF JESUS' BIRTH: ANGELS AND SHEPHERDS COME FROM LUKE, AND WISE MEN AND KING HEROD FROM MATTHEW.

In other ways, the stories are quite different. Luke tells of John the Baptist, the angel Gabriel's appearance to Zechariah and Mary, the faith of Elizabeth, the presence of shepherds, Simeon and Anna in the Temple in Jerusalem, and the great canticles or songs of praise. But Matthew says nothing of these. Instead, he speaks of Joseph who, apart from Jesus himself, is the main character in his birth stories — Joseph, the dreamer, just like his namesake in the Old Testament (Gen 37–60).

Matthew tells the story of the coming of the Magi, wise men from the East, whose arrival at the court of King Herod leads to the massacre of the male babies in Bethlehem. He tells of Jesus' flight into Egypt and his eventual resettlement in Nazareth. There are no songs in his account. Instead we find a series of quotations from the Old Testament, showing how the events of Jesus' birth fulfil the hopes and dreams of God's ancient people, Israel.

Matthew begins his Gospel in a most unusual way — at least, to our ears. He commences with the genealogy of Joseph (1:1–18), the father of Jesus. This begins with Abraham, moves to David, and concludes with Joseph himself. Matthew divides the genealogy neatly into three groups of fourteen generations (though the maths doesn't quite work).

This may seem an odd way to begin, not just the story of Jesus, but the whole of the New Testament. But Matthew has a point to make. Here, and elsewhere, he anchors the story of Jesus firmly in the Old Testament. Jesus belongs to Israel and arises from Israel. His presence indicates the faithfulness of God to his covenant.

There is an unusual feature to this genealogy. Matthew inserts the names of four women into a male-only list of descendants, from Abraham to Joseph. The first woman is Tamar, who seduced her father-in-law, Judah, since he had seriously wronged her (1:3; Gen 38). The second is Rahab, a Canaanite prostitute, who assisted the children of Israel to destroy the city of Jericho (1:5a; Josh 2). The third is Ruth, a Gentile, who married the Israelite Boaz in order to care for Naomi her mother-in-law, and became the great-grandmother of King David (1:5b; Ruth 1–4). The fourth is Bathsheba, the wife of Uriah, who married David after having an affair with him, and made sure her son, Solomon, became the next King (1:6; 2 Sam 11–12). No single factor unites these women. But they are all depicted in the Old Testament as women of courage, who do unusual and even countercultural things. They point forward to the fifth woman, the most unusual and courageous of them all: Mary of Nazareth, who becomes the mother of the Messiah (1:16).

There is another unusual feature of Matthew's genealogy. At the end of the long list of 'begettings', God bypasses the male biological line altogether, so that Joseph is not the father of Jesus, but rather the husband of Mary 'from whom the Messiah was born'. God uses human history but is also equally capable of bypassing it to achieve His ends.

> 2 Abraham was the father of Isaac, and Isaac the father of Jacob, and Jacob the father of Judah and his brothers, 3 and Judah the father of Perez and Zerah by Tamar, and Perez the father of Hezron, and Hezron the father of Aram, 4 and Aram the father of Aminadab, and Aminadab the father of Nahshon, and Nahshon the father of Salmon, 5 and Salmon the father of Boaz by Rahab, and Boaz the father of Obed by Ruth, and Obed the father of Jesse, 6 and Jesse the father of King David … 16 and Jacob the father of Joseph the husband of Mary, of whom Jesus was born, who is called the Messiah.
> (Matthew 1:2–6, 16)

Yet Joseph is, in every sense, a true father to the infant Jesus. His courageous decision to marry his pregnant fiancée, on the basis of a dream (1:18–25), and his consistent care for mother and child throughout the infancy story reveal his true character. He is kind, caring, intelligent, and wise: gifts much needed by this vulnerable child who has already made fearsome enemies. Despite his initial doubts, Joseph marries the young woman who is carrying a child that is not his. Yet his care as an adopted father, guided throughout by God, is the reason Jesus survives his childhood. Joseph puts the safety of the child and his mother above everything else (2:13–15, 19–3).

These days, people are sometimes sceptical of the story of Jesus' miraculous conception, arguing that it goes against nature or that it means Jesus is not fully human. But that is not Matthew's view (or Luke's). For Matthew, it is Mary who ensures the full humanity of Jesus. Yes, his birth happens through divine intervention, but it is also thoroughly human. As a baby, Jesus is as defenceless and needy as any other newborn.

LUKE'S ATMOSPHERE IS FULL OF JOY IN HIS BIRTH STORY, WHEREAS MATTHEW'S IS A MORE SOBERING STORY.

The real point is that Jesus' identity is a complex one. From his mother, and his mother alone, he gains his humanity: his full humanity. But his birth is also the direct work of the Spirit (1:20). In one sense, Jesus is the same as we are. In another sense, he is different from us: the one and only Son of God. The virginal conception is Matthew's way (and Luke's) of expressing that Jesus Christ is both human and divine.

The story of the coming of the Magi seems, at first glance, a delightful aspect of Matthew's story (2:1–12). The church usually celebrates their arrival at Epiphany on 6 January. These wise men are Gentiles, from outside Judaism, astrologers who read in the stars of the birth of this wondrous child. They travel a long distance to find Jesus and take mistaken turnings to get there, but they are overcome when they finally see the child and his mother: 'When they saw that the star had stopped, they were overwhelmed with joy' (2:10). This is a moment of great joy in Matthew's story. As we read, we share the happiness of the wise men as they bend the knee to worship the infant King.

But their story is also a terrible one. In the midst stands Herod the Great with his neurotic paranoia. The wise men, naturally enough, first take their enquiries to Herod, but in retrospect no decision could have had worse consequences (2:1–2). Discovering Bethlehem as the place of the Messiah's birth, Herod consults the magi to discover the details, pretending to share their enthusiasm (2:3–8). A number of baby boys are massacred in Bethlehem as a consequence of his paranoia. Matthew is acutely aware of the suffering, especially of the mothers (2:16–18).

This grief points forward to the ending of Matthew's story. Just as the Magi point to the coming of the Gentiles to faith, so the massacre of the Innocents hints at the crucifixion, the massacre of God's own Son. His enemies do not lay hands on him as a baby, thanks to his father's careful vigilance, but in the end, as an adult, they do get him. The slain babies of Bethlehem share their fate with the Son of God, as he shares theirs.

In all this, Matthew emphasises the events of Jesus' birth as the fulfilment of God's promises in the Old Testament. Five times throughout the story Matthew quotes from the Old Testament to show how Jesus brings the biblical story to fruition (1:23 [Isa 7:14], 2:6 [Mic 5:2], 2:15 [Hos 11:1], 2:18 [Jer 31:5], 2:23 [Judg 13:5]). While the biblical events have their own meaning, in their own context, they also have an extended meaning, pointing forward to Jesus.

Matthew's birth story is a dark, brooding one, full of danger, doubt, and violence. There are moments of light, but there is also a profound awareness of the reality of the world into which the Son of God is born. Though Christmas is a time of joy, it is also a time to face the reality of the world, and its desperate need for redemption. Jesus is born precisely as the Saviour. In him, God embraces our humanity with all its ugliness and sin. He does so in order to save us from it, to transform the world into a place of beauty, peace and goodness.

That is the meaning of Jesus' coming for Matthew.

> ONLY MATTHEW AND LUKE TELL OF JESUS' BIRTH FROM A VIRGIN. IT SHOWS THAT JESUS IS DIVINE, AS WELL AS HUMAN.

Jesus Prepares for his Ministry: Matthew 3:1–4:23

After the birth stories, Matthew turns his attention to Jesus' adult life. The first two chapters show us Jesus' preparation for that ministry (Matt 3–4). They also show something of Jesus' identity and mission, which will occupy most of the succeeding chapters of this Gospel. Here Matthew picks up Mark's narrative from its beginning (see Mk 1:1–20).

As with the other three Gospels, Jesus' ministry begins, not with himself, but with the preaching and baptising of John the Baptist (3:1–12). In Matthew, the first thing we hear is John's proclamation: 'Repent, for the kingdom of heaven has drawn near!' (3:1). This is the same message which Jesus himself will proclaim (4:17, 23). In Matthew, Jesus and John the Baptist are very close, proclaiming the same good news and enduring, eventually, a similar fate.

The term 'kingdom of heaven' needs explanation, as it is unique to this Gospel. In the first place, Matthew often has a preference for 'kingdom of heaven' over 'kingdom of God'. This illustrates how very Jewish Matthew is. Although he can and does speak of the 'kingdom of God', as the other Synoptic Gospels do, he prefers to avoid the divine name in this phrase, most likely out of respect.

> **Matthew tends to avoid the phrase 'kingdom of God' and prefers to use 'kingdom of heaven'.**

In the second place, the word 'kingdom' is a slightly misleading term in English. In the original Greek, 'kingdom' signifies the reign or rule of God. It is not so much a place as an activity: the gracious, sovereign activity of God. We are invited to enter this place of mercy and goodness.

As with Mark, John's ministry stands in the tradition of the prophet Elijah, as his strange clothing and lifestyle indicate (3:4; see 2 Kgs 1:8). John's message may seem harsh, with its images of judgment, but it is meant as purifying or cleansing so that people may prepare themselves for the Coming One.

Unlike Mark, Matthew tackles head-on the question of why Jesus himself is baptised. Why should he need cleansing or repentance of any kind? But Jesus insists on being baptised along with everyone else (3:13–17). When John the Baptist objects, he replies, 'it is proper for us to fulfil all righteousness' (3:15). Jesus does not need to be baptised, but his coming is precisely to identify with sinful humanity in need of repentance. He lives as one of us, prepared to do what we need to do, prepared to live as we should live.

Later, Matthew's Jesus will speak of coming to fulfil the Law in his own person. In the baptism we see the beginning of that journey of humiliation, where Jesus takes the humble path, the path of obedience.

Yet Jesus' baptism is not like anyone else's baptism. As he arises from the water, an epiphany takes place: the Spirit appears in the form of a dove, and the Father speaks, attesting to Jesus as the Beloved Son (3:16–17). In this momentous scene, all three Persons of the Trinity are revealed. Jesus possesses an extraordinary identity as the Son, and God's favour lies on him and his ministry.

It may seem strange that the first thing Jesus does is to go out into the harsh wilderness (4:1–11). We might expect the Beloved Son to be cared for and nurtured. Instead the Spirit leads him out to come face-to-face with evil. He is tempted by the devil in three ways (which are not found in Mark).

First, Jesus is tempted to trust in his own power rather than that of God (4:3–4). Secondly, he is tempted to prove God's care of him by a spectacular demonstration (4: 5–7). And thirdly, he is tempted to gain power and authority by worshipping the Devil rather than God (4:8–10).

In the first two temptations, the devil says, 'If you are the Son of God ...' That is exactly what is being tested here. Will Jesus behave as *the Son*, which he has just been proclaimed as at his baptism, or will he fail the test? In the period of the exodus, the children of Israel spent forty years wandering in the wilderness, failing to trust in God's care of them, complaining and rebelling. But where those sons and daughters of God failed, Jesus the true Son succeeds.

1 Then Jesus was led up by the Spirit into the wilderness to be tempted by the devil. 2 He fasted forty days and forty nights, and afterwards he was famished. 3 The tempter came and said to him, "If you are the Son of God, command these stones to become loaves of bread." 4 But he answered, "It is written, 'One does not live by bread alone, but by every word that comes from the mouth of God.'" 5 Then the devil took him to the holy city and placed him on the pinnacle of the temple, 6 saying to him, "If you are the Son of God, throw yourself down; for it is written, 'He will command his angels concerning you,' and 'On their hands they will bear you up, so that you will not dash your foot against a stone.'" 7 Jesus said to him, "Again it is written, 'Do not put the Lord your God to the test.'" 8 Again, the devil took him to a very high mountain and showed him all the kingdoms of the world and their splendour; 9 and he said to him, "All these I will give you, if you will fall down and worship me." 10 Jesus said to him, "Away with you, Satan! for it is written, 'Worship the Lord your God, and serve only him.'" 11 Then the devil left him, and suddenly angels came and waited on him.
(Matthew 4:1–11)

We often think of the Temptation showing Jesus as a model for resisting temptation. But that's not the primary meaning. For Matthew, Jesus in the wilderness has forged a new path for us. He has remade our disobedient, distrustful, wayward humanity and, this time, got it right. In his temptations, faced with the power of evil, he stays true to himself and his identity, and true to his God.

In the process of doing so, Jesus remakes our humanity, making it possible for us to face temptation and overcome it: not just because Jesus is a model for us, but because he has already achieved our humanity for us, on our behalf. His obedience can now become ours. We can claim it as our own.

Now that the Temptations are over, and Jesus is revealed as the true Son of God in his actions, his ministry can begin. As with Mark, that ministry begins in Galilee (4:12–17). Matthew uses a quotation from Isaiah 9:1–2 to emphasise that Galilee is particularly significant for the shape of Jesus' ministry. In the first century AD, Galilee had a number of towns in which mostly Gentiles lived, while in the countryside the inhabitants were mainly Jewish. Galilee, therefore, was a place of mixed race. Matthew draws attention to this. Galilee is the place of the Gentiles (as well as Jews) where the light of the good news dawns on those who live in darkness, whether physical or spiritual.

Jesus' first action is to gather a community around him. He calls the first four disciples—later apostles—to follow him and live a life of radical obedience and self-giving (4:18–22). In many ways, this incident shows what it means to *repent*. Repentance, for Matthew, is not primarily about feeling sorry for sins. It is much more concerned with transformation: a change of heart and lifestyle. That is what we find in the disciples' immediate response; they do not hesitate but turn and follow him. We too receive the same summons and call.

> MATTHEW IS THE MOST JEWISH OF THE FOUR GOSPELS. HE HAS A STRONG COMMITMENT TO THE LAW OF MOSES AND TO THE TRADITIONS OF THE OLD TESTAMENT.

As we see in the following chapters, Jesus' ministry is two-sided. It consists of preaching and teaching, on the one hand, and healing, on the other. This dual ministry of word and deed is characteristic of Matthew. In both senses, through teaching and healing, Jesus brings the good news of God's reign to those in need. That too is the church's vocation.

Jesus' Ministry in Word and Deed: Matthew 5:1–16:12

The Sermon on the Mount is perhaps the most famous passage in Matthew's Gospel (5:1–7:27), and the first of the five discourses. Luke's Gospel has a parallel in the 'Sermon on the Plain' but it is much shorter (Lk 6:17–49). Some of the other sayings from the Sermon on the Mount are scattered through Luke. Matthew probably gathered various sayings of Jesus together to form the Sermon, based on one or more sermons of Jesus himself, who probably used these sayings on more than one occasion. Neither sermon is found in Mark.

We tend to associate the Sermon on the Mount with the Ten Commandments, as the great guide to moral living for everyone, not just Christians. After all, it contains such marvellous sayings as the Golden Rule, 'In everything do to others as you would have them do to you;' (7:12), which is sensible advice for everyday living.

But the Sermon on the Mount is more than ethical guidelines. It is equally concerned with spirituality. Perhaps outlining the structure makes clear this concern with moral and spiritual living. The Sermon begins with the Beatitudes (5:3–12), with their focus on spirituality, and ends with the Parable of the Two Foundations (7:24–27), which has a distinctly ethical ring. At the centre of the Sermon stands the 'Our Father', the Lord's Prayer (6:9–13).

The Beatitudes have a balanced structure and set out the spirituality of discipleship, of following Jesus. Each saying presents a group of people who are 'blessed' in the eyes of God and who will receive God's future blessings. Their closeness to God and to divine values is assured. Their values are the opposite of what the world promotes.

The 'blessed' are aware of their dependence on God, they long for the righteousness (the goodness and justice) of God's reign, they do not have ego problems, they grieve for the state of the world and work for peace, they are single-minded in their devotion, and often persecuted for what they believe and the way they live. Their spirituality is dynamic, revealing the gracious dominion and rule of God. They are truly God's children.

As the Sermon progresses, we see that Jesus has a positive attitude towards the Law of Moses (5:17–20). The Law does not disappear with the coming of Christ. On the contrary, Matthew's Jesus fulfils the Law. He interprets it in a way that places love and mercy at the centre, but still upholds it. Following Jesus, therefore, means accepting the Law as Jesus interprets it, possessing a goodness and integrity that exceeds that of many religious leaders, who do not practise what they preach.

This 'better righteousness' is set out in a series of five balanced sayings — often called *antitheses* — which compare previous interpretation with Jesus' own (5:21–48). To follow Jesus in his interpretation of the Law means not just keeping it in external things, but also the heart. Thus, to hate someone breaks the commandment against murder; to lust after someone is to break the commandment against adultery. Our love is to be so complete that we can even love our enemies. We are to be like God and treat others with the same impartial goodness which God shows (5:45).

The middle section of the Sermon has a strong focus on spirituality, as well as ethics (6:1–34). It begins with prayer, fasting and almsgiving (caring for the poor). These are to be practised out of genuine love and piety, not in order to gain status before others. The Lord's Prayer exemplifies what genuine goodness means: reverencing God; longing for God's kingdom; depending on God for all our needs, physical and spiritua; forgiving others as God has forgiven us and being kept from all forms of evil.

> 7 "When you are praying, do not heap up empty phrases as the Gentiles do; for they think that they will be heard because of their many words. 8 Do not be like them, for your Father knows what you need before you ask him. 9 Pray then in this way: Our Father in heaven, hallowed be your name. 10 Your kingdom come. Your will be done, on earth as it is in heaven. 11 Give us this day our daily bread. 12 And forgive us our debts, as we also have forgiven our debtors. 13 And do not bring us to the time of trial, but rescue us from the evil one." (Matthew 6:7–13)

Once our hearts are right before God, everything else falls into place. We are to treasure and trust God, living without anxiety and with faith in the Father's providential care (6:25–34). With this, we are to become kinder and more just (7:1–5): less judgmental of others and more concerned for their wellbeing.

We are also to be people of discernment: not easily led astray or deluded (7:15–23). We are to assess our leaders on the basis of their works. If the fruit is good, then so too is the tree. It is a frightening thought that not everyone who claims to belong to Jesus demonstrates this level of commitment by their life; not everything called by the name of 'Christian' can be trusted.

And all this, Jesus concludes, is to be the rock on which disciples build their lives, the rock which is the Law, reinterpreted and lived out by Jesus himself. Without such a foundation, their lives have no constancy or centre. They stand on sinking sand.

In all this, Matthew is clear that, as Christians, we need guidance for living. But such guidelines are empty and impossible to achieve without a deep sense of spirituality: a trust in and love of God, grounded in prayer. Indeed, law without spirit, for Matthew, is dangerous. The directions of the Sermon on the Mount are intended to be liberating for the church, not constricting and life-denying. They are the banks of the river which enable the water to flow.

The chapters following the Sermon on the Mount are mostly focused on Jesus' miracles (7:28–9:38). Each story is short and succinct, displaying Jesus' profound compassion for those who are distressed in body and mind. Each story also shows the faith of those who come for healing and release.

Thus Jesus heals a leper, declaring him clean and fit to rejoin society (8:1–4). He heals a Roman soldier's servant and is amazed at his faith, seeing him as a sign of the future coming of the Gentiles (8:5–13). These are outsiders whose faith is sometimes greater than that of the insiders. Peter's mother-in-law, along with many others, is healed (8:14–17), and a storm is calmed on the sea for the terrified disciples in the boat (8:18–27).

> IT IS IMPORTANT THAT WE TAKE SERIOUSLY THE DIFFERENCES BETWEEN THE GOSPELS, IN ORDER TO HEAR THE DISTINCTIVE VOICE AND MESSAGE OF EACH.

Matthew uses another source in common with Luke, often called the 'Q' source, which was mainly sayings of Jesus.

JESUS' MINISTRY IN WORD AND DEED 21

Jesus casts demons from two demon-possessed men in Gentile territory, demons that are so powerful they destroy a herd of pigs (8:28–34). He heals a paralysed man, to the fury of the authorities, enabling him to walk (9:1–8). Later, in a combined story, he heals a woman who has a menopausal disability and raises a young girl from death (9:18–26). Last of all, he heals disabilities of sight and sound: two blind men, who show remarkable faith, have their eyes opened, while a mute man is empowered to speak (8:32–34).

Matthew sees the words of Isaiah 53:4 fulfilled in Jesus' healing miracles: 'He took our infirmities and bore our diseases' (8:17). We usually read these words in the context of Jesus' Passion, but Matthew understands them to be of Jesus' ministry. His mighty acts show that he is the true Servant of God, because he takes away people's suffering, embodying in his ministry the liberating mercy of God.

These chapters are also concerned with discipleship, and what it means to follow Jesus. The calming of the storm encourages the disciples to trust even when things seem out of control: in the tumult of trouble and persecution (818–27). The paralysed man is not only healed in body but also in soul: his disability is overcome, as his sins are forgiven (9:1–8). Jesus' table-sharing with sinners emphasises that his coming is for those who are spiritually 'sick' and in need of welcome and salvation (9:9–13). Jesus' power over long-term illness and death encourages faith in the reader, even in the extremities of human experience (9:18–26).

At each point, Jesus is motivated by compassion: for the needy and the sick, the leprous, the demon-possessed, and the disabled. In Jesus' eyes, says Matthew, they are 'harassed and helpless, like sheep without a shepherd' (9:36). It is to such a harvest of human need that the labourers are required, who will carry out Jesus' own ministry of healing and wholeness.

The second of Matthew's five discourses is the Mission Discourse (10:1–42). Here Jesus sends out the twelve apostles, whom he has just appointed, on mission, the same mission as his own: to heal the sick, cast out demons, raise the dead, and proclaim the reign of God. They are sent with little more than the power of the message: no suitcase, money, or extras of any kind. Not only are they to proclaim and heal; they are also to live the life of evangelical poverty which Jesus himself lives, and which authenticates the message.

Oddly enough, Jesus instructs them to go only to villages and people in Israel. They are to avoid Gentiles altogether. Matthew here is confirming the priority of Israel in God's saving plan. In the end, the good news is for Gentiles as well as Jews, but in the first place it goes to 'the lost sheep of the house of Israel' (10:6).

Jesus accompanies his instructions to the Twelve with warnings. The mission will be fraught with danger. Violence will not always come from outsiders but often enough from families. Despite the liberating message of the good news, it sometimes gives rise to hostility rather than reconciliation: a sword rather than peace (10:34). The ultimate aim of God's reign is to bring peace, but not everyone desires God's good news, and sometimes they will go to any length to stifle it.

The apostles are assured of God's presence. They are following the path of Jesus himself, and they are identified entirely with God. The way people respond to their mission is telling: to accept the mission is to accept Jesus

> MATTHEW DOES NOT SET 'LAW' OVER AND AGAINST 'GRACE' IN HIS GOSPEL. FOR HIM, THEY BELONG TOGETHER. FOR HIM, THE LAW OF MOSES HAS AT ITS HEART 'MERCY AND JUSTICE AND FAITH'.

himself and God; to reject it, and the messengers, is to reject God.

Jesus has demonstrated his own mission in word and deed, in teaching and healing. He has also handed over this authority to the apostles. Thus when John the Baptist in the next chapter asks the key question, 'Are you the one who is to come, or are we to wait for another?' (11:3), Matthew's Jesus is able to answer with a resounding 'yes' (11:4–6).

In affirming his identity, Jesus assigns no blame to John for his doubts. On the contrary, Jesus praises him in the highest terms (11:7–15). John is a prophet in the tradition and likeness of Elijah. In the first century, many people thought Elijah would one day return to announce the arrival of the kingdom (11:14).

Yet both Jesus and John have been discarded (11:16–19). No matter how different their lifestyle—John's harsh and self-denying, Jesus' social and communal—they have been rejected. In particular, Jesus focuses on the towns of Galilee who have not responded to his ministry (11:20–24). He compares them to cities with a legendary reputation for corruption, cities that would have repented under such a ministry.

At the end of the chapter is one the most beautiful passages from Matthew, which has given comfort to Christians all down the generations (11:25–30). Jesus begins by thanking the Father for revealing the good news, not to the wise and knowing, but to the little people: those considered of no account in the eyes of the world. In words that are reminiscent of the Gospel of John, Matthew indicates the intimate relationship that exists between the Father and the Son (11:25–27).

Yet this same Jesus, who alone can reveal the Father, is also 'gentle and humble in heart' (11:29; see 5:5). In this lowly guise, he calls people to discipleship. The invitation is addressed specifically to those who 'are weary and carrying heavy burdens' (11:28). Matthew has particularly in mind those burdened by a harsh and legalistic interpretation of the Law.

Instead they are offered the 'yoke'—that is, the teaching—of Jesus, which is easy, well-fitting, light and restful. This 'rest' has overtones of the sabbath in the Old Testament, with suggestions of the life to come. To follow Jesus, to strive for the kingdom and its righteousness, is paradoxically the one and only place to find peace and life.

> 25 At that time Jesus said, "I thank you, Father, Lord of heaven and earth, because you have hidden these things from the wise and the intelligent and have revealed them to infants; 26 yes, Father, for such was your gracious will. 27 All things have been handed over to me by

my Father; and no one knows the Son except the Father, and no one knows the Father except the Son and anyone to whom the Son chooses to reveal him. 28 Come to me, all you that are weary and are carrying heavy burdens, and I will give you rest. 29 Take my yoke upon you, and learn from me; for I am gentle and humble in heart, and you will find rest for your souls. 30 For my yoke is easy, and my burden is light." (Matthew 11:25–30)

Jesus' attitude to the Law as life-giving is powerfully illustrated in the following two stories, which both concern the sabbath (12:1–14). In the first story, Jesus defends the disciples picking grain on the sabbath on the grounds that the heart of the Law is 'mercy and not sacrifice' (12:7; Hos 6:6). Being 'Lord of the Sabbath' (12:8), Jesus alone can rightly interpret its meaning.

Similarly, when he is presented with a disabled man in the synagogue, Jesus decides to heal him on the sabbath, on the grounds that it is right to show mercy on the sabbath according to the Law (12:11–12). In this way, Jesus shows himself to be the true Servant of God, the one in whom the Spirit dwells, who gives hope and healing to all (12:15–21).

At the same time, Jesus' liberating interpretation of the Law, grounded in compassion and mercy, gives rise to hostility. Those in power are challenged by his teaching and ministry. They want to kill him (12:14), they attempt to discredit him by ascribing his power to Satan (12:22–32), and they challenge him for a sign that they are unlikely, in any case, to believe (12:38–42).

Jesus defends himself against the absurdity of their accusations. He shows that his ministry is the work of God's Spirit, signifying not the presence of evil but, on the contrary, the reign of God (12:28). He warns his own generation of God's judgment, seeing their lack of compassion as the door to great evil.

In the end, Jesus is left with his own disciples, who are his true family: those who share the same love and longing for God's will (12:46–50).

The Parables of Jesus (13: 1-53) represent the third of Matthew's great discourses. Many of these come to Matthew from Mark's Gospel, but some are Matthew's own additions. There is a distinctly agricultural theme to the parables. Most are to do with growth and become metaphors for the kingdom of God.

Two of the parables are included with an explanation by Jesus, which probably comes from the early church's later reflection on their meaning. The Parable of the Sower is originally a tale of extraordinary harvest at the end of remarkably difficult sowing (13:3–9). This is metaphorical for the unexpected joy with which God's reign comes to us. Matthew interprets this parable as an allegory of different responses to the message of the kingdom. Only those whose roots are deep can endure, and bear fruit (13:18–23).

In general, parables are enigmatic and express something of the mystery of God. Many will refuse the effort to understand—but others do see and hear, and their state is indeed blessed (13:16–17). Yet parables, Matthew emphasises, are not meant to confuse; their intention is to reveal 'what has been hidden from the foundation of the world' (13:34–35).

The second parable that adds its own explanation is the Parable of the Weeds among the Wheat, which is unique to Matthew (13:24–30). The wise farmer allows the two to grow side by side, since the type of weed here resembles wheat in its early stages. As Jesus explains it, this parable is an allegory of the world, with its jumble of good and bad mixed together, the wheat planted by God and the weeds by the Devil (13:36–43). At the end of time, there will be a final sorting, where evil will be cast out, and only the good will remain (13:36–43).

The same theme of final judgment emerges in the last parable, the Dragnet, which pictures the end of the age like fishermen sorting their catch, the good fish from the bad (13:47–50).

Matthew pairs two small parables of growth: the Mustard Seed and the Yeast (13:31–33). In both, something very ordinary happens which is also, at the same time, extraordinary. A tiny seed is planted and grows into a tree, a haven for birds. A small amount of yeast is mixed into dough, and the bread rises to form a loaf. From what is small and hidden, the kingdom of God grows mysteriously into something big and wonderful.

Perhaps the most beautiful of the parables are the paired Parables of the Treasure and the Pearl (13:44–46). These two show how the kingdom draws us in and transforms us. In the first, someone finds treasure by accident; in the second, the finder is already seeking the 'pearl of great value'. In both, the main characters sell everything in order to gain the desired object. Likewise, the kingdom calls us to give everything we have in order to find it: the one treasure above all others.

> 44 "The kingdom of heaven is like treasure hidden in a field, which someone found and hid; then in his joy he goes and sells all that he has and buys that field. 45 Again, the kingdom of heaven is like a merchant in search of fine pearls; 46 on finding one pearl of great value, he went and sold all that he had and bought it. 47 Again, the kingdom of heaven is like a net that was thrown into the sea and caught fish of every kind; 48 when it was full, they drew it ashore, sat down, and put the good into baskets but threw out the bad. 49 So it will be at the end of the age. The angels will come out and separate the evil from the righteous 50 and throw them into the furnace of fire, where there will be weeping and gnashing of teeth. 51 Have you understood all this?" They answered, "Yes." 52 And he said to them, "Therefore every scribe who has been trained for the kingdom of heaven is like the master of a household who brings out of his treasure what is new and what is old."
> (Matthew 13:44–52)

Matthew concludes this discourse with the image of the scribe who draws new and old from his treasure chest (13:51–53). Some have suggested that this is a picture of Matthew himself, the Christian scribe, drawing together Jesus' teaching (the new) and the Old Testament traditions (the old) in order to communicate the dynamic presence of God's reign.

The irony is that, at the end of this great block of teaching, with its fine imagery and profound meaning, Jesus receives nothing but rejection from home (13:54–58). His teaching causes friends and neighbours to take offence. As a consequence, the lack of faith elicits few miracles from him.

In the section which follows (14:1–16:12), Matthew follows Mark's Gospel fairly closely. These chapters focus on the imagery of bread, which wends its way through all the incidents described, but in particular the two feeding stories.

We begin with the banquet for Herod's birthday, at which John the Baptist's head is presented on a platter to Herodias, the wife of Herod, and her dancing daughter (14:1–12). This story of royal indifference, revenge, and murder is another tragic note in the otherwise uplifting tale of Jesus' successful ministry.

It makes sense that Jesus now wants to withdraw after receiving this news: to be alone and to pray. But the enthusiastic crowds follow him relentlessly (14:13). Jesus' response to their determined pursuit is not frustration and anger but compassion for their needs. He heals them and shows concern for their hunger at the end of the day. The same mobbing of Jesus and his generous response is also apparent at the end of the first feeding story (14:34–35).

The feeding begins with two small loaves (not much bigger than bread rolls) and two fish—at most a meal for one person (14:13–21). Yet it feeds more than 5000 people and what is left over, in twelve baskets, vastly outweighs the original quantity. Matthew here, like Mark, sees overtones of the End-time banquet, when all will sit down at table in the reign of God, with generous supplies of food and drink.

But there also distinctly eucharistic themes. Jesus looks up to heaven, blesses and breaks the loaves, and gives them to the disciples to distribute to the people. Similarly, at the Last Supper, Jesus takes the bread, blesses and breaks it, and gives it to his disciples, with the words, 'Take, eat; this is my body' (26:26). For Matthew, Jesus continues to 'feed' us with his body and blood, giving us a foretaste of the final banquet in the kingdom of God.

As with all the feeding accounts in the four Gospels, the feeding itself is followed by a boat scene, as the disciples return to Galilee. On this occasion, told only by Matthew, when Jesus comes to them on the sea, Peter goes out on the water to meet Jesus. Confronted by the winds and the waves, he loses faith and begins to sink, and is rescued by Jesus' strong hand (14:21–28).

The story is a parable of Christian living. While we continue to keep our eyes on Jesus, we can brave all kinds of 'storm' and difficulty. Once we lose focus, we begin to flounder, and only Jesus, the divine Son of God, can save us.

The next two incidents continue the imagery of food, but also deal specifically with issues of ritual cleanliness (15:1–28). In the first case, Jesus becomes involved in conflict over ritual laws concerned with eating. The concern about the disciples eating with unwashed hands has nothing to do with health, according to the standards of the day. In the ancient Jewish world, the issue has to do with ritual laws and the requirement for ritual purity.

As we might expect from Matthew's Jesus, there is no dismissal here of the Law; rather, it is reinterpreted. Jesus does not try to defend his disciples. Instead he goes on the attack, with an example of how the authorities try to

> MATTHEW OFTEN PUTS PARABLES TOGETHER, NOT BECAUSE JESUS ALWAYS TOLD THEM IN GROUPS BUT BECAUSE IT WAS AN EASY WAY TO REMEMBER THEM IN ORAL TRADITION.

get around the Law, so that they do not need to support their aged parents (14:3–9). Their role as guides on matters of the Law is undermined by their hypocrisy. Jesus goes on to redefine what 'clean' and 'unclean' mean, and he does so in moral and ethical terms.

The real defilement comes not from what goes into the mouth, but rather what comes out. It is the heart and its words and actions that have the capacity to defile: 'evil intentions, murder, adultery, fornication, theft, false witness, slander' (14:21).

Significantly, this incident is followed by the approach of an unclean woman, who asks Jesus to cast the demon from her daughter (15:21–28). The woman is a Gentile; Matthew calls her a 'Canaanite', recalling the past enemies of Israel in the Old Testament. Jesus seems to dismiss her, and his disciples attempt to silence her, but to no avail. Though an outsider, she uses the language of the insiders: 'Have mercy on us, Lord, Son of David' (15:22). She accepts the insult about 'bread' being only for Israel—accepts that she is a Gentile 'dog' (dogs being unclean animals)—but she turns the imagery around: even the dogs eat the crumbs under the table (15:27). This extraordinary faith moves Jesus to heal her daughter.

This scene marks an important turning-point in the Gospel. To this point, Jesus' mission in Matthew has been mostly directed at 'the lost sheep of the house of Israel' (10:6, 15:24). Now, with this luminous example of Gentile faith, the outsiders—the unclean—demonstrate a faith to rival Israel. With the Canaanite and her faith, the doors open beyond Israel. The Gospel here reflects the mission of the early church, which found an astonishing openness to the good news among Gentiles.

The scene is followed by the second feeding story, which bears remarkable similarities to the first (15:29–6:12). Once again, we witness Jesus' compassion for sick and suffering people, including those suffering from hunger. With a small quantity of food, Jesus again feeds the hungry, with a large amount left over. As with the first, there are overtones of the final banquet and the eucharist. Once again, the scene ends with a boat journey.

This time, Jesus attempts to warn the disciples of the religious leaders. He uses the imagery of yeast, not positively as in the Parable of the Leaven (13:33) but negatively, as a symbol of the hidden way evil can grow. It is ironic that the disciples, only half-listening to Jesus and misunderstanding him, are fussing instead over their lack of food (16:7). Jesus reminds them of the feedings, and points to the spiritual and metaphorical meaning of yeast.

Unlike the disciples in Mark, Matthew's disciples do grasp his message and comprehend what Jesus is saying: in this case, his warning against the evil that hides behind a mask of uprightness. Matthew encourages them, and us, in our stumbling attempts to follow Jesus. Our faith may not be as strong as we think it ought to be, but it is still faith and we can hold to Jesus, who feeds us with his word, with his body and blood. What we cannot be is blind to the reality of evil around us, especially when that evil emerges from within the community of faith.

Jesus' Journey to Jerusalem: Matthew 16:13–20:34

At 16:13, a significant change occurs in the direction and focus of Jesus' ministry. This scene at Caesarea Philippi, and the scene that follows on the mountain, form the centre of Matthew's Gospel, as in Mark's (16:13–17:13; see Mk 8:27–9:13). Jesus begins by confronting his disciples with the question of his identity. He does so in two stages. First, he asks for the views of other people on this question, and secondly he directs the question to them (16:13–15).

> 13 Now when Jesus came into the district of Caesarea Philippi, he asked his disciples, "Who do people say that the Son of Man is?" 14 And they said, "Some say John the Baptist, but others Elijah, and still others Jeremiah or one of the prophets." 15 He said to them, "But who do you say that I am?" 16 Simon Peter answered, "You are the Messiah, the Son of the living God." 17 And Jesus answered him, "Blessed are you, Simon son of Jonah! For flesh and blood has not revealed this to you, but my Father in heaven. 18 And I tell you, you are Peter, and on this rock I will build my church, and the gates of Hades will not prevail against it. 19 I will give you the keys of the kingdom of heaven, and whatever you bind on earth will be bound in heaven, and whatever you loose on earth will be loosed in heaven." (Matthew 16:13–19)

It is important to note that this scene does not represent a crisis of identity for Jesus himself. The question is didactic, a teaching device, giving Matthew's Jesus the opportunity for further revelation on the question of his identity and destiny.

In Mark's account, though Peter answers accurately enough, a question-mark hangs over his confession of faith. While he knows the right answer, he has no idea of its implications (Mk 8:29–33). In Matthew, however, Peter's answer, which is more effusive than in Mark, is right: 'you are the Messiah, the Son of the living God' (16:16). Jesus declares that it is the result of revelation and not Peter's own insight. Peter is, indeed, among the 'blessed' because he has spoken under divine inspiration.

MATTHEW CALLS JESUS 'THE CHRIST', WHICH IS THE SAME AS 'MESSIAH' AND MEANS 'ANOINTED ONE'.

Peter's confession of faith also leads Matthew in a different direction to Mark. Whereas in Mark, Jesus immediately reveals his coming suffering, death and resurrection (Mk 8:31), the Matthean Jesus first declares the founding of the church. A scene concerned primarily with the revelation of Jesus' identity in Mark, becomes, in Matthew's hands, the revelation of the church.

This church is founded on Simon Peter, the first stone (though not the cornerstone, which is Jesus himself, 21:42), and on his understanding of who Jesus is. Jesus' statement is a pun, a play on words: 'rock' is *petra* in Greek, directly related to the name *Petros* (the pun also works in Aramaic, the language spoken by Jesus and his disciples). Clearly, 'Peter' is a nickname given to Simon by Jesus himself. In John's Gospel, Simon is named 'Peter' at his first meeting with Jesus (Jn 1:42).

In the Old Testament, certain individuals are given a change of name. A new name, for example, is given to Abraham (from 'Abram' to 'Abraham', Gen 17:1–8), and also to Jacob ('Israel', Gen 32:22–32). In each case, the change relates to the people of God. The same is true here. Like Abraham (and Sarah), Peter is the 'rock from which you were hewn' and the 'quarry from which you were dug' (Isa 51:1). As Abraham was blessed by God in being the father of Israel, so too is Peter.

The word 'church' (*ekklêsia*) is used here for the first time in the Gospel (16:18), and is found twice more in Matthew (18:17). Nowhere else in the four Gospels is the word used, although it is common elsewhere in the New Testament (Acts, Paul, Revelation). This rare usage in the Gospels makes it stand out the more in Matthew, indicating its centrality in this passage. For Matthew, this is the founding moment of the church, as decisive for him as Pentecost is for Luke (Lk 24:49, Acts 1:4–5; 2:1–13).

In founding the church, Matthew's Jesus also gives Peter the 'keys of the kingdom' and authority to 'bind and loose' (16:19). The authority of binding and loosing is later given to the whole church (18:18).

The image of the keys, granted only to Peter, is not easy to interpret. There are many jokes in our culture of Peter standing at the gates of heaven, allowing (or not allowing) entry into Paradise. These are based on a common misunderstanding: that Peter holds the power to give or withhold entry into heaven. But it is unlikely that the keys refer to entry into heaven. They signify the bunch of keys held by the household steward who needed to have access to all the rooms and storage places in the house. This is not unlike the role of a butler in well-to-do households in past generations. Peter's role is that of a superior servant within the household, who has the trust and authority of his master.

It is hard to know what is meant by the authority to 'bind and loose'. Some people think it refers to the power of exorcism given to the disciples (10:8): the power to cast out evil. Others think it refers to the teaching authority of the church, as in the Great Commission at the end of the Gospel (see 28:19). Still others think it means the ability to forgive sins and exercise discipline within the church (see 18:15–35). In Jewish circles, binding and loosing referred to the authority to give moral and spiritual guidance on the Law.

Most likely, Matthew is presenting Peter as the chief Rabbi who holds teaching authority in the community. This authority may include discipline and forgiveness. Matthew's point here is that the decisions made by Peter and the whole church are to be ratified by heaven itself. The church in Matthew is not the same as the kingdom of heaven, but there is a direct link between them: the one points to the other.

It is ironic that, as the scene progresses, Peter shows a very different form from that of the rock. Now he attempts to turn Jesus from the way of suffering, even though Jesus makes it plain that the journey he takes is at God's command ('he *must* go to Jerusalem', 16:21). Peter's language is

> PETER PLAYS A KEY ROLE IN MATTHEW'S GOSPEL. HE IS THE ROCK OF THE CHURCH, BUT ALSO THE ONE WHO DENIES JESUS THREE TIMES. HE IS THE TYPICAL DISCIPLE — FULL OF FAITH, ONE MINUTE, AND DOUBTING THE NEXT.

forceful, but even more remarkable is Jesus' identification of Peter, at this moment, with Satan who stands in the way of God's reign (16:23).

Peter is thus both the rock of the church but also the one who can impede God's way. Throughout the Gospel, Matthew presents Peter in a dual role of strength and wisdom, insight and delusion, courage and fear. In more ways than one, Peter represents the church and the typical disciple. We see our own image reflected in that of Peter: our insights and our failings all together in the one place, yet embraced by Christ's calling. Like Peter, we are called *for* who and what we are; and we are called sometimes *in spite of* who and what we are.

In the face of Peter's misunderstanding, Jesus explains to the disciples what it really means to follow him (16:24–28). The path of the church is not triumphalist, but the way of self-denial and suffering for the sake of others, for the sake of the gospel. This is the path of life, the journey to Jerusalem that Jesus takes, leading to his future return in glory and the journey that all disciples are called to follow.

This central scene at Caesarea Philippi is immediately followed by the Transfiguration (17:1–13). Both incidents together lie at the heart of Matthew's Gospel. Although Matthew follows Mark at this point, he tells the story in his own way. Jesus climbs a high mountain with his three closest apostles: Peter, James and John. There he is changed and his full identity revealed, along with the presence of Moses and Elijah, two key prophetic figures from the Old Testament, both associated with mountains and revelation.

1 Six days later, Jesus took with him Peter and James and his brother John and led them up a high mountain, by themselves. 2 And he was transfigured before them, and his face shone like the sun, and his clothes became dazzling white. 3 Suddenly there appeared to them Moses and Elijah, talking with him. 4 Then Peter said to Jesus, "Lord, it is good for us to be here; if you wish, I will make three dwellings here, one for you, one for Moses, and one for Elijah." 5 While he was still speaking, suddenly a bright cloud overshadowed them, and from the cloud a voice said, "This is my Son, the Beloved; with him I am well pleased; listen to him!" 6 When the disciples heard this, they fell to the ground and were overcome by fear. 7 But Jesus came and touched them, saying, "Get up and do not be afraid." 8 And when they looked up, they saw no one except Jesus himself alone. (Matthew 17:1–8)

Matthew's language is full of symbols of light. Jesus' face shines like the sun and the cloud that overshadows them is bright and blazing with light. This splendour reveals Jesus' identity as the divine Son, a splendour that stands in the tradition of—yet far exceeds—the greatness of Moses on Mount Sinai, whose face also shone (Exod 34:29-35).

And just as the voice of God acclaims Jesus at his baptism (3:17), so now the same voice confirms Jesus at this turning-point in his ministry, as he begins his journey to Jerusalem. The dazzling cloud is suggestive of the Spirit, who descends on Jesus at his baptism, making this a second trinitarian moment in the Gospel.

Matthew is equally concerned with the vocation of the church, which is represented particularly in Peter, for all his misunderstanding. Jesus approaches the overawed disciples with tenderness and understanding, and raises them up with reassuring words (17:7). He shows compassion for their misunderstanding.

We too, like the three disciples on the mountain, are drawn into Jesus' Transfiguration. This event reveals not only Jesus' identity but also our future destiny. We too, with them, will be 'transfigured' into the likeness of the Lord.

After the disappearance of the heavenly signs—Moses and Elijah, the light, the cloud and the voice—and during the descent down the mountain, Jesus reveals to the disciples that they have witnessed a vision of God's future. This vision is transmitted from the past by Moses and Elijah, and from the future by the majestic yet compassionate figure of Jesus, the Beloved Son. It radiates our present and sets us within the orbit of God's final reign.

Duccio di Buoninsegna, *The Transfiguration*

As Jesus tells the disciples as they descend the mountain, the messenger of the kingdom, as it is embodied in Jesus himself, is John the Baptist (17:9–13). John is an Elijah figure, whose violent end is itself a sign pointing to Jesus' own Passion.

The theme of Jesus' identity, his Passion, death, resurrection and future glory, run centrally through these two episodes: the revelation at Caesarea Philippi and the revelation on the mountain. Who Jesus is as the Beloved Son and his journey from death to life, from humiliation to glorious exaltation, stand at the very heart of Matthew's story.

Jesus' descent of the mountain pushes him at once into the reality of human suffering and limitation. He is confronted by a demon-possessed boy and his father, as well as the inability of the disciples to heal (17:14–20). Yet the power to heal needs only human faith, even though only the smallest speck is needed to ignite it.

The disciples' lack of faith is accompanied by a lack of understanding. For the second time, Jesus announces his death and resurrection, leaving the disciples in uncomprehending grief (17:22–23). They have not yet grasped, any more than Peter has, the nature of Jesus' journey.

Matthew now prepares us for the fourth of his great homilies, the Community Discourse. It is preceded by a strange incident in which Jesus agrees to pay the temple tax, finding the coinage miraculously in the mouth of a fish (17:24–27). Yet the paying of this tax, says Jesus, is not an obligation but done out of a desire to avoid offence. The freedom of 'the children' sets the scene for the discourse that follows, which deals with life among the children of the kingdom (18:1–35).

The discourse begins with a kind of enacted parable in which Jesus illustrates what true greatness means in the reign of heaven. The child Jesus places before the disciples embodies the attitude of true disciples, which is one of humble dependence on God (18:1–4). Children, in this sense, are

> THE TRANSFIGURATION STANDS AT THE HEART OF MATTHEW'S GOSPEL, JUST AFTER HE REVEALS WHO HE IS REALLY IS AND ANNOUNCES THE FOUNDING OF THE CHURCH.

models for disciples: we are to imitate their simple trust. At the same time, this illustration outlines the church's pastoral role which is directed towards these 'children', who are to be welcomed in the name of Christ (18:5).

Matthew's Jesus is speaking metaphorically, at least in part. Not only children but all the ordinary people, without pretensions to wealth, power, or status, are included in the phrase 'little ones'. To harm one such 'child', to place a hurdle before their wellbeing, is to open ourselves to judgment. These 'little ones' are the 'blessed' of the Beatitudes (5:3–12), who are special before God, and stand in contrast to any in the community, especially leaders, who might abuse them. Here 'woe' is the opposite of 'blessed'.

The values required of leaders in the church in their dealings with God's children in the church are to be evident in their lives. Not only are they to care, lest no stumbling bar the way of a disciple, but they are also to ensure that no such obstacle stands in their own way (18:8–9). Discipleship, and leadership, in the church requires personal self-sacrifice: not for its own sake, but to promote the flourishing of life. This is not unlike the image from John's Gospel of the vine-grower pruning the vine, cutting off dead branches to enable the plant to thrive (Jn 15:2).

Matthew now turns, more explicitly, to the theme of caring for the 'little ones' in the community whose wellbeing is a matter of concern to the citizens of heaven, as the beginning and end of this small section makes plain (18:11, 14). The image used is, literally, one of pastoral care. Luke too uses this parable in his Gospel, although his interpretation is focused on Jesus' own mission (Lk 15:3–7).

> BOTH MATTHEW AND LUKE TELL THE PARABLE OF THE LOST SHEEP. IN LUKE, IT RELATES TO JESUS' OWN MINISTRY TO TAX COLLECTORS AND SINNERS. IN MATTHEW, IT DESCRIBES THE PASTORAL WORK OF THE CHURCH.

For Matthew, the Parable of the Lost Sheep demonstrates the attitudes and behaviour of Christian pastors (18:12–13), who are to go to extravagant lengths in their care of the sheep, especially the lost. Perhaps, in this parable, we see ourselves in both: with the shepherd caring for the lost, and also among the lost ones, the 'little ones', in need of homecoming and care.

From the theme of pastoral care, Matthew moves to the issue of conflict among disciples (18:15–20). The language here is that of family: 'member of the church' should read 'brother or sister'. Jesus offers a simple and practical method of dealing with conflict, which involves confronting rather than avoiding the issue. The one who feels wronged should confront the issue with the offending brother or sister: at first privately, to seek repentance, then with witnesses, and finally the whole church should be involved.

It may seem harsh that Jesus proclaims that the unrepentant sinner should be treated as 'a Gentile and a tax collector' (18:17). There is no doubt that, in the past, such statements have been used to exclude people unjustly. But Matthew is suggesting that, if we refuse to acknowledge the harm we have caused another, in a sense we exclude ourselves: we have moved out of the realm where forgiveness is given and received.

Matthew underlines the church's authority to create such a place of forgiveness with the imagery of 'binding and loosing', first used regarding Peter (18:18; see 16:19). This is the authority of God's people as a whole and requires only two or three to be authentic. Here the church is constituted not primarily by hierarchy but by the ingathering of Jesus' disciples who share the same desire for the reign of heaven. Extraordinary as it may seem, the risen Christ is present wherever we, as his people, are gathered together. Matthew will reinforce this point at the very end of his Gospel (28:20b).

The last section of the discourse deals explicitly with the theme of forgiveness which is, for Matthew, a central feature of the church's life (18:21–35). Peter proposes seven times as a generous limit on forgiveness but Jesus radically expands the number: 'not seven ... but seventy-seven times' (18:22). This leads into the Parable of the Unforgiving Servant (19:23–35). Jesus tells this parable to show the absurdity of receiving forgiveness while refusing to forgive. The parable draws a contrast between the 10 000 talents owed by the servant to his master, and the 100 denarii, a minute sum in comparison, which his fellow-slave owes him. Yet, while receiving forgiveness of the large sum, he refuses to forgive the small one.

As with the Lord's Prayer (6:9–13), Jesus uses the imagery of debts for sin. The metaphor suggests that there are things such as goodness, integrity and justice ('righteousness', as Matthew would say), which we, in a sense, 'owe' to God and one another. Failure to offer goodness makes us indebted to the other, whether divine or human. Yet the liberating message of the good news is that God cancels our debts, freely and generously, while at the same time summoning us to live with the same generosity and readiness to cancel the 'debts' owed to us.

Once again, the refusal to forgive alienates us from the church, which is to be the realm of forgiveness and mercy. If we cannot ask for or receive forgiveness, we are in danger of placing ourselves outside that circle of mercy. It is true that neither of these things is easy. Sometimes all we can do is pray for the ability to forgive and be forgiven, and sometimes we need to ask forgiveness for our inability to forgive and be forgiven. That includes the capacity to forgive ourselves. It is God's forgiveness that sets the tone for ours.

The next section of Matthew's Gospel deals with several related issues concerning domestic life and labour (19:1–20:16). Here Matthew explores the values and spirituality of the reign of heaven. Most of the material comes from Mark's Gospel, but with significant additions and editing by Matthew himself (see Mk 10:1–34).

Matthew begins with the question of divorce, which was a contentious issue in ancient Judaism. In some forms of Jewish thinking, women could be divorced for trivial reasons, and sent home to their father's house in disgrace and without their children. As in Mark's Gospel, Jesus takes a much more serious view of divorce, a view we have already encountered in the Sermon on the Mount (5:31–32). The question is not an honest one (19:3): Jesus' opponents are trying to discredit him.

In the following discussion, Jesus seems to be setting the provisions of the Old Testament ('Moses', e.g. Deut 24:1–4), which permit divorce, against the order of creation which sees marriage as a profound and lasting union of persons (Gen 1:27, 2:24). What Matthew is asserting, however, is the deeper principle undergirding the Law, which allows for exceptions. Marriage is intended to be a rich and abiding union between two people for their lives, which no one should be allowed to disrupt. Elsewhere, as we have seen, Matthew acknowledges the human realities of marriage and the need for exceptions. On this point, Matthew is unique among the Synoptic Gospels.

Matthew also is unique in allowing another exception: not everyone need marry. There is a place for celibacy in the life of the community, he argues, and for any number of reasons (19:10–12). The ancient Jewish world, in particular, placed great emphasis on marriage. Here Jesus makes marriage a choice rather than a social obligation.

Matthew's theology of discipleship is centred on ordinary, everyday life, affecting all that we do in our lives. Children too are welcomed by Jesus, though not so enthusiastically by his disciples (19:13–15). Not only does Jesus pray over them, he also declares that 'to such as these ... the kingdom of heaven belongs' (19:14). This welcome extends to all who are childlike, those who are prepared to 'change and become like children' (see 18:3). The child and the childlike adult are equally welcome in heaven's domain.

From marriage and children, Matthew passes on to the issue of wealth (19:16–30). Here again, Jesus' attitudes surprise his contemporaries, including his disciples. The rich young man who approaches Jesus has not come to discuss his wealth. His concern is, pure and simple, with spirituality and ethics. How should he live in order to find life? This is a variant, in Jewish terms, of the perennial question of the meaning of life. Jesus answers the question at face value, giving a Jewish answer: keep the commandments (19:18–19). But, for the young man, this is not enough; something is still missing. Jesus responds with a staggering suggestion: that he give away his possessions to the poor in order to find the 'treasure in heaven' his heart craves. But he cannot do so, and leaves in grief.

Jesus' own sorrowful reflections on this episode astonish his disciples. How can wealth be anything but a sign of God's blessing? But, for Jesus, wealth can equally well be a barrier that impedes access to God. In this case, the young man is being called to cut off a hand or foot, or pluck out an eye in order to find life (see 18:8–9). His wealth prevents him finding the one thing he desires and needs.

The disciples take comfort, in the end, from Jesus' words. They may find the economy of the kingdom strange and topsy-turvy—the last first and the first last—but they know too that they have surrendered everything to follow Jesus (19:27–30). For Matthew, nothing given up for the gospel will be lost, no sacrifice unrewarded, no generous act unacknowledged. The challenge for us is to ask what impedes our entry into the kingdom: what stands in our way?

Lastly, in this section, Matthew raises the issue of labour in the Parable of the Labourers in the Vineyard, found only in this Gospel (20:1–16). The link with the previous story (despite the unfortunate chapter division) is made clear by the repetition of 'the first will be last, and the last first' (19:30, 20:16). Jesus presents a typical situation in ancient Palestine, with day labourers waiting in the marketplace, hopeful of employment. The landowner hires labourers in five shifts throughout the day. In the end, he pays them all the same wage, despite the fact that some have worked all day and others only for the last hour. The landowner responds to the objections by pointing out that he has not wronged them. Their envy is the problem not his management style.

The parable is not a recipe for industrial relations. But it does point to the power of God's mercy and God's refusal to regard what we consider the ordinary decencies of life. There is no injustice done, and yet ... how many of us would feel differently? But God's goodness does not follow our human instincts. It follows its own delightful path: never unjust, but often unpredictably and undeservedly generous, even extravagant. To belong in the kingdom is to belong in this crazy world, where human values are stood on their head and everything seems the wrong way round.

Two further incidents bring to a close Jesus' journey to Jerusalem. Both follow the Markan story. In the first, Jesus proclaims for the third time on the journey his coming death and resurrection (19:17–19). Far from understanding, the disciples show that their priorities—their human values—are seriously askew. It is the brothers James and John (as in Mark's account, Mark 10:35–45), but their mother who approaches Jesus to ask for the best seats for her sons in the coming kingdom (20:20–21). Jesus promises the boys a share in the cup he will drink—which will turn out to be the cup of suffering, not at all what their mother intended—but no more, as the authority is not his but the Father's (20:22–23).

> 20 Then the mother of the sons of Zebedee came to him with her sons, and kneeling before him, she asked a favour of him. 21 And he said to her, "What do you want?" She said to him, "Declare that these two sons of mine will sit, one at your right hand and one at your left, in your kingdom." 22 But Jesus answered, "You do not know what you are asking. Are you able to drink the cup that I am about to drink?" They said to him, "We are able." 23 He said to them, "You will indeed drink my cup, but to sit at my right hand and at my left, this is not mine to grant, but it is for those for whom it has been prepared by my Father." 24 When the ten heard it, they were angry with the two brothers. 25 But Jesus called them to him and said, "You know that the rulers of the Gentiles lord it over them, and their great ones are tyrants over them. 26 It will not be so among you; but whoever wishes to be great among you must be your servant, 27 and whoever wishes to be first among you must be your slave; 28 just as the Son of Man came not to be served but to serve, and to give his life a ransom for many." (Matthew 20:20–28)

The anger of the other apostles demonstrates their equal misunderstanding. Jesus presents them with a model of leadership which, once again, overturns social expectations. Jesus himself is the model of true authority. As the Son of Man, his death is the ultimate act of leadership and it demonstrates, not hierarchy, status or social order, but rather self-giving service (20:24–28).

A footnote to this story is that, whereas James and John are absent from the crucifixion, their mother is standing at a distance, in company with the other holy women (see 27:56). It would seem that she, at least, in the end gets the point. The Book of Acts also recounts that James was later martyred (see Acts 12:2).

In the final episode, the theme of discipleship comes again to the fore (20:29–34). Jesus, in his compassion, grants healing to two blind men sitting by the roadside. At once they follow him, joining the company of disciples as Jesus enters Jerusalem. For us to follow Jesus, in Matthew—as in the other Synoptic Gospels—means following his journey to the cross: to death and resurrection.

Jesus' Days in Jerusalem: Matthew 21:1–25:46

The final chapters of Jesus' ministry in Matthew focus on the theme of conflict and revelation. Matthew continues Mark's story in this section, but with a number of additions. Most significantly, he expands Mark's apocalyptic discourse (Mk 13) into his fifth and final discourse, with additional parables and sayings which are uniquely his own.

The story of Jesus' Triumphal Entry into Jerusalem is a splendid moment in the Gospel narrative, and something of that joy often emerges in our Palm Sunday celebrations (21:1–11). The event takes place at Jesus' own initiative (21:1–3) and, according to Matthew, in fulfilment of the Old Testament (21:4; Zech 9:9). The quotation makes it plain that Jesus enters the city, not in triumph on a war horse, but on a domestic animal, an animal of peace. Matthew, however, mentions two animals, the donkey and its colt. His reference to Jesus sitting on them both (21:7) is probably not to be taken literally: wherever the mother animal goes, so does her offspring.

The spreading of cloaks and leafy branches is an expression of joy and reverence. Most significant is the crowds' acclamation, using words from Psalm 118:26: 'Hosanna! Blessed is he who comes in the name of the Lord...' (21:9). The procession ends in the temple, which Jesus cleanses, removing all signs of trade and money changing, in order to restore it to its intention as 'a house of prayer' (21:13; Is 56:7). Here too Jesus heals the sick and disabled, people traditionally excluded from the temple. Something new is happening, a new intolerance for dishonesty and greed; a new sense of inclusion for those on the outside.

Neither the healings nor the 'hosannas' of the children impress the authorities and so the conflict of that final week begins. It centres around the temple, where Jesus returns the next day, having cursed the barren fig tree on the way (21:18–22). This is a strange incident, which Matthew takes from Mark (Luke judiciously omits it) and uses as an object lesson in faith.

From now till the end of chapter 22, Jesus engages in hostile debate with the authorities in the temple, where he defends himself and also goes on the attack (21:23–22:46). They begin by questioning the source of his authority, a question he answers with another question that they refuse to answer on the grounds it will incriminate them. Jesus' authority is from heaven, just as John the Baptist's was (21:23–27).

Note here that the crowds' enthusiasm for Jesus protects him from his enemies (21:46). At this stage, the authorities are attempting to discredit his teaching before the people. Later, they will need to use devious means to arrest him and have him condemned.

The conflict continues with three parables, aimed largely at the authorities but also in part at those who have followed him. In the first, which is unique to Matthew, Jesus contrasts two brothers in the Parable of the Two Sons (21:28–32). One of them appears to do the right thing but does not in the end, while the other is rebellious but ends up doing what

> 'Hosanna' originally is a cry for God to save us. By the time of the Gospels, it has become a cry of praise, like 'Alleluia'.

he should. Jesus explains the parable as an allegory of the hypocrisy of the Jerusalem authorities in comparison to the 'tax collectors and prostitutes': the outsiders who finally, unlike the authorities, carry out the will of God. Jesus claims outrageously that they, rather than the religious leaders, have priority in God's reign.

The second parable, which all three Synoptics have, is a more blatant attack on the authorities, and they have no difficulty in recognising it as such (21:33–44). The vineyard is a common Old Testament image for Israel. In this potted 'history' of Israel, Jesus criticises its leaders for their inability to honour the covenant and God's demands for justice and goodness (the 'fruits' of the vineyard). Jesus identifies himself with the prophets, sent again and again to bring the leaders to a sense of their injustice. He, however, is not simply another prophet or servant; this time it is the son and heir whom God sends, yet who suffers the same fate as the others.

Ironically, the tragic and cruel fate of the son will be the very means God uses for his own purposes: the death of Jesus, rejected and cast out, will prove to be not a tragic disaster, but rather the 'cornerstone' of the new community (21:42; Ps 118:22–23). The people who will 'produce the fruits' and who will replace the leaders is most likely, for Matthew, a reference to the Gentiles.

The third in the series is the Parable of the Wedding Feast (22:1–14). Matthew makes the allegorical meaning plain. The wedding feast is based on Old Testament imagery of the final banquet at the end of time, when the kingdom of heaven will be fully realised. Matthew sees that event already set in motion in Jesus' ministry. The guests prove unworthy of the invitation, with their weak excuses, and so all the outsiders are invited instead: the poor, the crippled, the blind and the lame. This is a marvellous parable of the generosity and inclusiveness of God.

But the parable has a strange and rather disquieting addition (21:11–14). One wedding guest, who has not bothered to avail himself of the correct attire, is cast out. Even the outsiders-become-insiders stand in a sense under God's judgment. It is most likely that Matthew sees the wedding garment as a metaphor for the good works that should be done by those invited into the kingdom. So there is a generous invitation, on the one hand, but there is also, on the other, a calling to uprightness and integrity of life: to justice and mercy and faith (see 23:23).

It is now the turn of the religious leaders to respond to Jesus' attack. They do so in a series of trick questions in an attempt to 'entangle him in his words' (22:15). The first question—asked by Pharisees—is a tricky one, fraught with political implications (22:16–22). To support the paying of taxes to the Roman imperial authority would alienate Jesus from the people; to oppose such payment would alienate him from the Romans. Jesus neatly side-steps the question with the puzzling statement: 'give ... to the emperor the things that are the emperor's, and to God the things that are God's' (22:21). This bewilders the authorities, and has continued to puzzle readers ever since!

The second question comes from another group within Judaism, the Sadducees. They pose a ridiculous scenario based on the Old Testament practice of a brother marrying his widowed sister-in-law to raise up children for his deceased brother (22:23–33). Here the intention is to attack common-held views on resurrection. Once again, Jesus steps lightly out of the trap and, in doing so, confirms the truth of the resurrection: marriage has no relevance in the coming reign of heaven and God *is*, not *was*, the God of Israel's ancestors (22:30–32).

> THE JEWISH PEOPLE OF JESUS' OWN DAY WERE VERY DIVERSE. PHARISEES AND SADDUCEES WERE JUST TWO GROUPS AMONG MANY, ALTHOUGH PROBABLY THE MOST POWERFUL.

> THE SADDUCEES RAN THE TEMPLE AND REPRESENTED THE UPPER CLASSES IN JERUSALEM. THEY ONLY READ THE FIRST FIVE BOOKS OF THE OLD TESTAMENT, AND SO DID NOT BELIEVE IN THE RESURRECTION.

The third question is another attempt to discredit Jesus by presenting him with a difficult theological question (22:34–40). Again it comes from the Pharisees, though in Mark's Gospel the same question is genuine (Mk 12:28–34). Here Jesus' answer gathers up the law into the simple equation of loving God and loving the neighbour as oneself, which for Matthew stands at the centre of all true religion.

Jesus now turns the questions on the Pharisees and asks them about the identity of the Messiah. He argues, on the basis of Psalm 110:1, that the Messiah is greater than David: David's son yet also David's Lord (22:41–45a). Jesus' clear victory in this public debate silences his enemies and no more questions are addressed to him. Now his enemies will use other, more vicious means to suppress him.

At this point, we might expect Jesus to be satisfied with what he has achieved and maintain a prudent silence. But such is not the case. Jesus is not interested in self-preservation. Once more he goes on the attack with a scathing denunciation of the scribes and Pharisees. The series of 'Woes' are the opposite, in some ways, of the Beatitudes. Whereas Beatitudes set forth those who are favoured by God, the Woes describe those who stand under God's judgment.

Before the Woes begin, Jesus introduces them by confirming that the scribes and Pharisees have a God-given responsibility for teaching the faith: they 'sit on Moses' seat' (23:2). Their teaching therefore is to be taken seriously, but not their actions which do not correspond to what they teach. They desire status in the community and parade their religiosity, being the very opposite of servant leaders (23:3–12).

In the Woes that follow, the religious leaders are condemned for failing in their God-given task. The issues Matthew tackles are their hypocrisy, their deliberate blindness, and their misreading of Scripture.

Thus, rather than enabling people to enter the kingdom, as they ought, the authorities actively lock them out (23:13–14). In making great efforts to win converts they end up polluting them (23:15). They misuse oaths in order to delude people (23:16–22; but compare 5:33–37 where oaths of any kind are forbidden). While they are scrupulous about details of the law (e.g. the tithing of garden herbs) they ignore the matters that really count: justice, mercy, faithfulness (23:23–24). Or, to use Jesus' vivid metaphor, they strain out small insects while swallowing whole camels.

In addition, says Jesus, they are concerned with external purity, but indifferent to inner vices such as 'greed and self-indulgence' (23:25–26). As a result, they seem good and pure on the outside, but are morally corrupt on the inside, putting on a hypocritical show of goodness that is entirely false (23:27–28). Like whitewashed tombs, they look good but are full of death. Finally, they honour their ancestors, the prophets and the righteous, but in fact their behaviour shows that they are at one with their persecutors (23:29–36).

This is a scathing denouncement that seems to become more and more passionate as it progresses. Yet it is important that we interpret the passage carefully and sensitively. Our context is very different from that of Matthew, and we need to make allowance for it. Most likely, Matthew is writing at a time when his main opponents were members of the Pharisaic party. In Jesus' own day, his friends and enemies alike were all Jewish and not confined to any one party within Judaism. We cannot read this passage as a tirade against Jewish people or even against all Pharisees.

What Matthew is condemning here is a type of leadership which is all-too-common in religious communities the world over, Christian included. It's a condemnation of leaders who lead people astray, who do not practise what they preach, who lose the wood for the trees, who become bogged down in legalistic details while ignoring the centre of their faith. It is a warning, in other words, for us.

At the same time, as the following passage makes plain, Jesus' tirade against blind leaders is accompanied by a profound sense of grief at the city of Jerusalem and its tragic rejection of God's messengers, including himself (23:37–39). His last words contain a note of hope. One day, the people of Jerusalem, led astray by their leaders, will yet welcome the One who 'comes in the name of the Lord' (23:39).

The last section before the Passion narrative is Matthew's fifth and final discourse (24:1—25:46). Matthew is again following but also expanding on Mark in these chapters. In particular, his expansion includes content not found anywhere in Mark's Gospel, including several parables. The discourse is Jesus' private farewell speech to his disciples, which is couched in strongly apocalyptic language and imagery, and in the context of prophecy concerning the destruction of the temple (24:1–2).

Apocalyptic literature is based on the notion that the present age is one of suffering and persecution while the future age will bring about the reign of God, the triumph of good over evil and the end of suffering and death. In this worldview, the days immediately before God's intervention will be a time of calamity, struggle, and suffering.

Matthew is strongly influenced by this apocalyptic perspective, as was Jesus himself. For Matthew, the new age has already begun in the ministry of Jesus. The terrible events Matthew depicts in this discourse describe not just the end of the world, but also prepare us for the Passion where much of this cosmic turmoil will begin.

The discourse as a whole is focused around two basic questions, asked by the disciples at 24:3 and answered in what follows (in reverse order): 'when will this be' and 'what will be the sign of your coming and of the end of the age'? The answer to the second question occupies 25:1–31 (What sign?). The rest of the discourse, 26:32—25:30 answers the first question (When?).

Matthew, following Mark, outlines a number of signs that will indicate the beginning of the end. There will be false and misleading signs which should not disquiet the community (24:4–8). There will be suffering,

> THE PHARISEES MOVED IN THE COUNTRYSIDE AMONG ORDINARY PEOPLE AND FOCUSED ON THE SCRIPTURES AND THE LAW.

betrayal and loss of faith (24:9–14). In addition, there will be an act of sacrilege within the temple by its enemies, and there will be fearsome consequences for those trying to escape the city (24:15–22). Warnings are issued against false prophets and Messiahs (24:23–28). Last of all, there will be cosmic disintegration (24:29).

Some of this language strikes us today as strange and even alien. It seems harsh, judgmental, and negative. But that is because we are not accustomed to apocalyptic language. In actual fact, the message is encouraging for the community, even in its direst warnings. The sufferings themselves are described as 'birth pangs' (24:8), the labour which precedes birth: in this case, the birth of God's wondrous reign.

Even the persecution will enable the spread of the good news, which is to be proclaimed 'throughout the world' (24:14). The days of suffering will be shortened for the sake of God's people (24:22). And, when the Son of Man appears in glory at the end of time, it will mean the final ingathering of God's people from all over the world and the end of all suffering (24:30–31; see Dan 7:13).

These signs should have the same effect on us as the signs of nature do. When the fig tree, for example, begins to sprout, the alert gardener recognises the signs of summer approaching (24:32–35).

The next part of the apocalyptic discourse focuses on the question of *when* these things will take place (24:36–25:30). To answer that question—inasmuch as it is answered at all—Matthew makes use of five parables or similes.

In the first two, Matthew calls the reader to vigilance. Admitting bluntly that only the Father knows the answer to *when* (24:36), Jesus recommends that the disciples instead focus on being watchful and vigilant. In Noah's generation, when people ignored the warning signs and continued with their lives as if nothing was happening, the flood took them disastrously unawares. If the householder had known the time of the thief's break-in, he would have stayed awake instead of going to bed. In both case, what was lacking was vigilance (24:36–44).

In the next three parables, the focus is on readiness and preparedness, a companion to vigilance. In the Parable of the Two Servants (24:45–51), one servant is prudent enough to prepare for the return of his master, and is scrupulously faithful to his duties. The other is careless, abusive of his responsibilities and his fellow-servants, with no preparation for his master's return.

The Parable of the Bridesmaids is not an easy parable to decipher, since we hardly know enough of the customs of the day to make complete sense of it (25:1–13). Yet the main point is clear enough. Some bridesmaids are prepared for a long wait for the wedding banquet and take extra supplies; the others are unprepared for any delay and are left out of the reception. Both parables contrast preparedness with unpreparedness, responsibility with irresponsibility.

In the third parable, that of the Talents, there is again a contrast between readiness and unreadiness, preparation and neglect (25:14–30). Two of the three servants who are given talents (whether five or two), make something of their master's wealth, doubling its value. The third servant buries his talent and makes nothing of it, apparently due to fear.

On the master's return, the first two servants are commended and rewarded, while the third is cast out. The language of reward and

> APOCALYPTIC IMAGES ARE COMMON IN MATTHEW'S GOSPEL. HE BELIEVES IN THE FUTURE KINGDOM WHICH WILL INVADE THE PRESENT AGE, BRINGING ABOUT GOD'S NEW AGE OF LOVE AND JUSTICE. YET THAT NEW AGE HAS ALREADY, IN ONE SENSE, DAWNED WITH THE COMING OF JESUS. IT WILL BE FULFILLED WHEN HE COMES IN HIS FUTURE GLORY.

punishment here seems excessive for the actual situation described. Yet Matthew is in apocalyptic mode, and his images are allegorical. The first two servants typify the faithful and committed disciple; the third represents the indifferent, the lazy, the irresponsible.

In these parables, Matthew is using language we associate mostly with Advent. Both vigilance and preparedness are to be part of the church's stance, as it turns its face, expectantly and joyfully, towards God's future. We too, as individual disciples, are called to live with the same joyful expectation and hope, not burying ourselves in our everyday lives as if nothing greater was to be expected or hoped for, but keeping alive in our hearts the longing for the kingdom, the reign of God, and for the end of suffering and death.

The last section of the discourse is one of the most majestic passages of Matthew's Gospel. Here Matthew concludes Jesus' ministry with an awe-inspiring vision of the Last Judgment, with the Son of Man exalted on his throne, engaged in the separation of the sheep from the goats (25:31–46).

The story has a clear pattern. The 'sheep' on the king's right are blessed and welcomed into the fold for their works of mercy; they exclaim in surprise, not knowing what they have done; the king explains that they have cared for the 'least of these who are members of my family' (literally, 'my brothers and sisters') and, in doing so, have cared for him (25:34–40). The same, in reverse, happens to the 'goats' on the left. They are cursed and asked to depart into 'eternal fire'; they exclaim in surprise, not knowing what they have done wrong; the king explains that they have neglected to care for 'the least' of his brothers and sisters, and have thus neglected him (25:41–45). There is a final conclusion, describing the opposite fate of each group: the goats to punishment, the sheep to life (25:46).

What is not so clear is why the righteous are unaware of the good deeds they have done. Mostly, this passage is taken as referring to God's judgment —whether positive or negative—on the church, where Christians are judged by their works for the poor and needy. It may be, however, that Matthew has in mind the judgment of the world, and how the world has treated the members of Christ's family. Either way, the message is a challenge for all disciples to live out their beliefs, especially in their care of the needy.

What is extraordinary in this passage is not just the challenge to mercy and compassion. Equally remarkable are the places where Jesus is located. On the one hand, he is exalted on the throne, the heavenly Son of Man, the King and Judge of all. On the other hand, he is also to be found among the poor and needy. He stands both at the centre and on the margins: above the high and mighty, and yet also in company with the lowly.

This paradox lies at the heart of Matthew's Gospel. Jesus is the lowly King, the One whose majesty is veiled, who stands in the place of God, yet who is present in the humblest, poorest, and lowliest of his disciples.

Jesus' Death and Resurrection: Matthew 26:1–28:20

Like so much else of Matthew's Gospel, the Passion story is closely connected to Mark's Gospel. Matthew uses Mark's basic structure and much of his content, while at the same time editing Mark and conveying his own message, which is uniquely his and not identical to that of Mark (26:1–27:66; see Mk 14–15).

Matthew's Passion story begins with Jesus predicting his coming death. This is Matthew's way of emphasising that the cross is part of God's plan and not a tragic mistake (26:1–2). It does not mean that God manipulates the situation, and the actors, to bring about the crucifixion. What it does mean is that God works in and through the apparent disaster. Far from thwarting the kingdom, the crucifixion in God's hands is transformed to become the means of salvation.

The first story in the Passion is that of the anointing (26:6–13). It is sandwiched on either side by the tale of the plot against Jesus by the religious authorities, a plot effected by the agreement of Judas Iscariot to betray him (26:3–5, 14–16). The contrast between the two stories is deliberate.

On the one hand, we have the spectacle of treachery among Jesus' closest disciples. On the other hand we find an unknown woman anointing of Jesus in an act of profound insight and love.

The woman acts as a prophet in anointing Jesus' head, and in recognising his forthcoming death. Her action and insight, Jesus says, become part of the proclamation of the good news. Note that the woman is nowhere identified with Mary Magdalene, nor is she a sinner in this story.

6 Now while Jesus was at Bethany in the house of Simon the leper, 7 a woman came to him with an alabaster jar of very costly ointment, and she poured it on his head as he sat at the table. 8 But when the disciples saw it, they were angry and said, "Why this waste? 9 For this ointment could have been sold for a large sum, and the money given to the poor." 10 But Jesus, aware of this, said to them, "Why do you trouble the woman? She has performed a good service for me. 11 For you always have the poor with you, but you will not always have me. 12 By pouring this ointment on my body she has prepared me for burial. 13 Truly I tell you, wherever this good news is proclaimed in the whole world, what she has done will be told in remembrance of her." (Matthew 26:6–13)

The next section of Matthew's Passion takes us through the events of Passover: its preparation, progression and aftermath. The preparations are orchestrated by Jesus himself, emphasising once again his sovereign control over events (26:17–19). At the meal, two unexpected things take place. To the disciples' dismay, Jesus' announces his betrayal and the identity of his betrayer (26:20–25). And he radically reinterprets the meaning of Passover.

Passover, for Matthew, now relates to Jesus and his death, as well as to the future life of the disciples (26–30). In the institution of the Eucharist, Jesus explains his death as a saving event, in which the future kingdom—'my Father's kingdom'—is experienced in the present by the disciples. The bread and the cup together signify the presence of Jesus himself and the covenant that is forged in his death, bringing about forgiveness, new life and a new relationship with God.

The aftermath takes place on the Mount of Olives, at the place where Jesus will be arrested. Jesus predicts the desertion of his disciples, with the striking of the 'Shepherd' (26:31–35). Yet this frightening prediction, which Peter strenuously resists, has also at its heart the promise of restoration in Galilee.

It is significant that the account of the Eucharist is surrounded by the betrayal and denial of the disciples: by their failure. Yet Matthew reinforces the message of forgiveness that lies at the heart of the Eucharist for the disciples and for us today.

Jesus immediately begins to prepare himself, through prayer, for the coming ordeal. He takes with him only his closest companions: Peter, James and John (26:36–46). There he reveals the intensity of his distress (26:37–38), and the depth of his own faith in God (26:39, 42). In contrast, the three disciples fail to support their Lord, or recognise their own danger. At the end of the scene, Jesus is ready to face betrayal and death, through the power of prayer, while the disciples are left unprepared.

The arrest makes this point plain, with its poignancy and violence (26:47–56). Jesus can accept his destiny, refusing either his disciples' attempts at violence or any form of heavenly rescue in order to fulfil the Father's will. His only reproach is to point out the deviousness of those who have not dared touch him in public (26:55). In contrast to his calm acceptance is the flight and desertion of the disciples (26:56).

Rembrandt, *The Descent from the Cross*

Following Mark, Matthew tells the story of what takes place in the high priest's residence as a contrast between inside and outside, between Jesus and Peter (26:57–75). Jesus is faced with false testimony that is so patently absurd that he does not deign to answer it (26:59–63).

In response to the high priest, Jesus answers enigmatically. Without directly affirming or denying his messiahship, he proclaims the future coming of the Son of Man, the Judge of the End-time, implying that that

JESUS' DEATH AND RESURRECTION 43

exalted figure is no less than Jesus himself (26:64; see Dan 7:13 and Ps 110:1). This is enough for the high priest to condemn Jesus and subject him to abuse and mockery (26:65–68).

By contrast, while Jesus confesses to his identity, Peter is outside denying his (26:69–75). After his three denials, which become more and vehement, Peter recalls Jesus' prediction and is overcome by his failure. Yet though he has failed his Lord, Peter at least has tried to follow him, and his repentance is perfectly genuine, enlisting our sympathy. Which is us would have fared any better?

Jesus is brought before Pilate, the Roman governor, to be tried and condemned (27:1–2, 11–26). Just as the trial begins, Matthew relates the story of Judas' suicide, brought on by a terrible sense of remorse at what he has done (26:3–10). How very different Judas' response is to that of Peter! Admittedly, Judas' act is much worse, but even his sin is not beyond the power of God's forgiveness: the seventy-seven times extends also to him (18:22). Instead of repenting, Judas chooses self-hatred and death. Matthew is the only Gospel writer who tells this story.

Pilate makes a feeble attempt to release Jesus during the trial, despite Jesus' silence in his presence and despite his own wife's solemn warning (26:19). But he is overruled by the determined religious leaders who promise anything to obtain what they want. Pilate instead washes his hands in a futile attempt to divest himself of responsibility for so blatant a miscarriage of justice. He releases a hardened criminal—Jesus Barabbas—while handing over Jesus the Messiah unjustly for crucifixion (27:15–26).

It is difficult to know what to make of the people's cry: 'His blood be upon us and on our children!' (26:25). It has often been interpreted to mean that responsibility for the death of Jesus has passed from Pilate on to the Jews, and thus, on to the Jews of future generations. This is a dangerous explanation, responsible for acts of antisemitism in the past. If it means that Matthew sees the Jewish people as a whole taking responsibility for Jesus' death, it is part of the tragedy of this event, that they are so grossly misled by their leaders. Responsibility for the death of Jesus resides primarily with the Romans and with Pilate (as the Creed makes clear).

> MATTHEW PLACES A GOOD DEAL OF EMPHASIS ON WOMEN THROUGHOUT HIS GOSPEL, OFTEN PRESENTING THEM AS FAITHFUL DISCIPLES OF JESUS.

On the other hand, it is possible that what the people are saying here, for Matthew, is more a plea that Jesus' saving blood will cover them and their children, despite these terrible events. If that is the case, they stand opposed to their leaders at this point in the story (as they have elsewhere in Matthew's Gospel).

One of the motifs of the crucifixion narrative in all the Gospels is that of the mocking of Jesus. The mocking emphasises the degradation and powerlessness of Jesus, as well as the fact that, in terms of the living world, he has lost all honour and has been publicly shamed. At one level, it is designed to humiliate Jesus even further but at a deeper level, it is profoundly true. When the Roman soldiers dress him up in kingly attire and mock him as a king, they reveal unintentionally the truth about Jesus (27:27–31). The charge over the cross—'This is Jesus, the King of the Jews' (27:37)—says it all. The crucifixion is ironically also an enthronement, where Jesus is revealed as King.

The Roman soldiers continue their role: they crucify Jesus and gamble for his clothing, while keeping guard lest any of his disciples try and rescue him. Jesus is now surrounded by cruelty, indifference and further degradation in the taunts of those around him, including his fellow-victims (27:32–44).

Once again, the taunts contain a deeper truth. Jesus will come down from the cross, but not before his death: rather in his glorious resurrection. And, yes, he did come to save others but not himself; that is his choice and also the will of God. In every way, Jesus shows himself to be the true, obedient Son of God who trusts utterly in his God and who will therefore be delivered.

Surrounding the death of Jesus are a number of apocalyptic signs, more than in any of the other Gospel accounts (27:45–54). First there is the three-hour darkness, not intended as a natural phenomenon, but rather signalling the looming presence of God's judgment. Then there is the reference to Elijah, the prophet of the End-time, though it is a mistake in hearing, as Jesus calls not on Elijah but on his God. Finally there is the tearing of the temple curtain, the earthquake, and the rising of the dead.

As the darkness lifts, Jesus cries out with a sense of God's absence, in words that are a quotation from Ps 22:1, 'My God, my God, why have you forsaken me?' God has not really abandoned his faithful and obedient Son, but desolation is the path Jesus has chosen to take: to drink to the full the cup of human suffering and anguish.

45 From noon on, darkness came over the whole land until three in the afternoon. 46 And about three o'clock Jesus cried with a loud voice, "Eli, Eli, lema sabachthani?" that is, "My God, my God, why have you forsaken me?" 47 When some of the bystanders heard it, they said, "This man is calling for Elijah." 48 At once one of them ran and got a sponge, filled it with sour wine, put it on a stick, and gave it to him to drink. 49 But the others said, "Wait, let us see whether Elijah will come to save him." 50 Then Jesus cried again with a loud voice and breathed his last. 51 At that moment the curtain of the temple was torn in two, from top to bottom. The earth shook, and the rocks were split. 52 The tombs also were opened, and many bodies of the saints who had fallen asleep were raised. 53 After his resurrection they came out of the tombs and entered the holy city and appeared to many. 54 Now when the centurion and those with him, who were keeping watch over Jesus, saw the earthquake and what took place, they were terrified and said, "Truly this man was God's Son!" (Matthew 27:45–54)

The apocalyptic signs are pointers to the meaning of this event for Matthew. The point is made clear by the Roman soldiers who proclaim his identity as Son of God, seeing the cosmic signs and overwhelmed by fear (27:54). This event represents the turning-point of the ages. It spells the end of the old order and the approach of heaven's reign. The tearing of the veil opens up the temple, the place of God's dwelling, to all people and not just the chosen ones. We are all invited to enter the holy place. It is, ironically, the death of Jesus which gives us access.

The raising of the dead is a strange addition to the story (not found in the other Gospels), and not easy to make sense of, especially if we try to interpret it literally (27:52–53). It too is part of Matthew's apocalyptic drama. It is as if resurrection itself bursts forth from the death of Jesus. His resurrection will result in the resurrection of the saints—although, oddly enough, in this incident, their resurrection precedes his. However clumsily expressed, Matthew's point is simple: the crucifixion, which speaks so loudly of death and disaster, is fundamentally about transformation and life.

Unexpected disciples now make their appearance at the scene. There are the holy women who, unlike the apostles, have neither deserted nor fled, but have followed Jesus faithfully from Galilee: Mary Magdalene, another Mary (who may or may not be the mother of Jesus, see 13:55), and the mother of the apostles, James and John (27:55–56). These women play an important role in testifying to these events, and two of them will also witness Jesus' burial (27:61).

The other unexpected disciple who now appears is Joseph of Arimathea (27:57–60). He has the status and wealth to gain *entrée* to Pilate and to bury Jesus in a proper tomb. The two women watch all that is happening. The guard at the tomb is set in place (27:62–66). All is now quiet.

The closing of the tomb and the sealing by the guard of soldiers closes Jesus' life utterly, from a human point of view. However, where human designs, hopes and intentions end, God's work is just beginning.

Matthew's resurrection story brings his Gospel to a dramatic climax. Mark has an ambiguous ending to his Gospel, with the women disciples fleeing the tomb in silence without meeting the Risen One (Mk 16:1–8), but Matthew enlarges Mark's story. There is no ambiguity in Matthew's ending. The story is joyfully resolved, the risen Christ appearing to the women disciples and to the apostles, in separate but parallel incidents (28:1–10, 16–20). In between these two resurrection appearances is the story of the guards at the tomb (28:11–15).

Unlike the other Gospels, the two holy women visit the tomb not to anoint the body but simply to 'see' it: to pay their respects and grieve (28:1). Matthew may well be conscious of the anointing of the woman at the beginning of the Passion narrative who has, says Jesus, 'prepared me for burial' (26:12). The anointing, in this sense, has already taken place. The whole of the Passion and resurrection is bounded, on either side, by the faithfulness and insight of these three women: the unnamed Anointer, Mary Magdalene and the other Mary.

One of the unique features of Matthew's account is that the rolling away of the stone takes place before the women's, and the guards', eyes (28:2–3). As at the crucifixion, there is again an earthquake, signifying the upheaval of the cosmos in the Easter events and the arrival of the heavenly messenger. This is the only direct appearance of an angel in Matthew's Gospel. In the Birth Narratives, the angel appears to Joseph only in dreams. But note

> MARK'S GOSPEL ENDS UNCOMFORTABLY, WITH THE WOMEN DISCIPLES RUNNING AWAY IN SILENCE FROM THE EMPTY TOMB. MATTHEW CHANGES THAT, SO THAT THE WOMEN CLEARLY BELIEVE. JESUS HIMSELF APPEARS TO THEM.

that, there too, the cosmos is affected: the heavens reveal the star at the beginning, and the earth shakes at the end.

Though the two Marys are frightened, they are nowhere near as terrified as the guards. The angel reassures the women, giving them the glorious message of the resurrection, showing them the empty tomb, and commissioning them to 'go quickly and tell' (28:5–7). The women respond at once in faith, in 'fear and great joy'; this time a holy fear, a reverence. On the way to carry out this command, they unexpectedly meet the Risen One who repeats the angel's reassurance and commission (28:9–10).

There is no actual need for this appearance of the risen Christ, except in confirmation of what has already taken place. Matthew, however, wishes to underline the importance of this scene at the tomb. In many ways, the women disciples exemplify what it means to be true disciples of Jesus: to be the church. Like them, we are called to believe, to worship and to proclaim the joyful Easter tidings in word and deed.

In the midst of this joy, we return to the guards' story and the fear of the authorities. So terrified are they of Jesus, even beyond the tomb, that they bribe the soldiers to claim that the body was stolen (28:12–13). Matthew is addressing an accusation in his own day, that Jesus never really rose from the dead. But this scene also emphasises the reality of the empty tomb and the importance of that tradition, based entirely on women's testimony.

The two Marys are obviously believed, because the Eleven go to meet the risen Christ. This great moment of revelation takes place, significantly, on a mountain and in Galilee (28:16). Mountains are places of revelation throughout Matthew's Gospel, as we have seen (e.g. 4:8, 5:1, 17:1), while Galilee is the place 'of the Gentiles', where Jesus' mission begins (4:12–17).

> NONE OF THE GOSPELS IS TRYING TO WRITE A JOURNALIST'S ACCOUNT OF THE CRUCIFIXION. EACH GOSPEL WRITER IS TRYING TO INTERPRET IT THEOLOGICALLY, DRAWING OUT THE MEANING FOR OUR LIVES AS DISCIPLES.

> MATTHEW GIVES NOTHING AWAY ABOUT WHERE OR TO WHOM THE GOSPEL WAS WRITTEN.

Like the two women disciples, the Eleven apostles worship Jesus, though there is still some doubt in their midst (28:17). Jesus commissions them for their mission as church. They are to 'go' to all the nations, including the Gentiles—they are to 'make disciples'; they are to 'baptize in the name of the Father and of the Son and of the Holy Spirit'; and they are 'teach' these disciples to obey Jesus' teaching (28:19–20).

These four commands lie at the heart of the church's mission. There is to be no exclusion in their mission: no in-group for whom the good news is intended, while leaving out everybody else. This message is for everyone, Jew and Gentile alike. Making disciples is, in fact, one word in Greek, a verb —'to disciple'—and there is no suggestion of coercion or manipulation. The gift of discipleship is to be offered freely.

Baptism means entry into the community. It is not a solitary activity but one that has communion and relationship at its heart. Here we find one of the few explicit references to the Trinity in the New Testament. It underlines that, in baptism, we are drawn into the relationship that exists between the Persons of the Trinity: created and recreated for love and relationship with God and one another.

Finally, teaching is a key aspect of the church's life. As we have seen throughout this Gospel, Jesus' teaching is as much about spirituality as it is about ethics. This is teaching, not just to instruct, but to nourish the soul.

It is not grounded on dry propositions but on a lively and dynamic theology, which is nurturing and life-giving.

The role of the church and of disciples is set out clearly in Matthew's conclusion to his Gospel. But this role is built on Christ himself, the cornerstone, the Lord of the church. These four commands are bounded on either side by declarations of Jesus' identity.

In the first place, they are based on Jesus' cosmic authority (28:18), an authority that the Devil offered him in the Temptation story and which he refused (4:8–10). For Matthew, Jesus has won this authority through obedience to God—by traversing the path of death and resurrection—and not through illegitimate means. It is therefore genuine, and it encompasses all of life and death. Christ is sovereign over the cosmic powers. There is great consolation in that for the church and for us, as disciples.

Statue of Christ the Redeemer, Corcovado mountain, Rio de Janeiro

Secondly, the Great Commission is based on the presence of the risen Christ (28:20). Not only does he send us forth, he also accompanies us on the journey, our constant companion and strength. He continues to be there 'in the midst' where two or three are gathered and where two or three are sent (see 18:20). The church's mission is his, under his authority and protection, as is the life of discipleship.

Here the Gospel of Matthew returns to its beginning. The birth of Emmanuel, 'God with us' (1:23), is now fulfilled in the resurrection and the abiding presence of Christ. He is 'God with us' to the end of the ages and the final fulfilment of heaven's reign. The two women disciples and the eleven apostles both testify to the presence of Christ; both groups worship him; both are commissioned with the joyful message.

Matthew invites their witness, their worship, and their mission to become ours, as we read and re-read this Gospel, so that we become truly 'children of your Father in heaven' (5:45) and faithful followers of his Beloved Son.